STAR QUILTS

35 blocks, 5 projects ▪ **Easy No-Math Drafting Technique**

Flying Facets, 45" × 38", 2012

Mary Knapp

C&T PUBLISHING

Text copyright © 2012 by Mary Knapp

Photography and Artwork copyright © 2012 by C&T Publishing, Inc.

Publisher: Amy Marson

Creative Director: Gailen Runge

Art Director: Kristy Zacharias

Editor: Lynn Koolish

Technical Editors: Janice Wray, Ann Haley, and Sandy Petersen

Cover Designer: April Mostek

Book Designer: Christina Jarumay Fox

Production Coordinator: Jessica Jenkins

Production Editor: S. Michele Fry and Joanna Burgarino

Illustrator: Aliza Shalit

Photography by Diane Pedersen and Cara Pardo of C&T Publishing, Inc., unless otherwise noted

Published by C&T Publishing, Inc., P.O. Box 1456, Lafayette, CA 94549

Library of Congress Cataloging-in-Publication Data

Knapp, Mary, 1946-

 Star quilts : 35 blocks, 5 projects - easy no-math drafting technique / Mary Knapp.

  pages cm

 ISBN 978-1-60705-657-7 (soft cover)

1. Patchwork--Patterns. 2. Quilting--Patterns. 3. Star quilts. I. Title.

 TT835.K562 2012

 746.46--dc23

                                      2012019275

Printed in China

10 9 8 7 6 5 4 3 2 1

CONTENTS

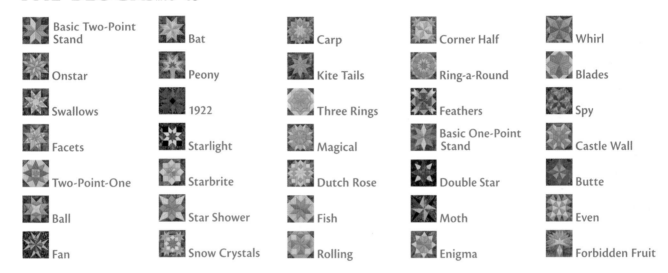
CUTTING AND PIECING TIPS AND TECHNIQUES...64

- Fabric Considerations ■ Working with Silk
- Making Templates ■ Cutting
- Piecing Techniques (*Piecing a Center Star, Piecing a Square or Triangle to a Center Star*)
- Paper-Guided Piecing ■ Block Piecing Guide
- Block Piecing Chart ■ Block Cutting Chart

PROJECTS

DEDICATION

To those students in fifth grade who said, "I can't draw."

To those students in tenth grade who said, "I can't do math."

To every three-year-old who has chosen an award-winning quilt to sleep under, just because "I liked it."

To every sibling who has ever put a picture of a sister and her quilt on the fridge.

And to individuals everywhere who say, "If I can listen to music and daydream, I can do anything."

ACKNOWLEDGMENTS

Thanks go first and foremost to my husband, Mike. He is the first one to answer my "What do you think about this color, this style …" questions. He has built every type of support stand possible to display my work for critical analysis.

I also depend on the input of my two sons, Marc and Jeff, and their families. As the initial viewers of my work, they are the first to see and trouble-shoot my projects and offer their opinions. I also have to thank my son Jeff and his wife, Rachel, for setting up and maintaining my website and my son Marc and his wife, Jennifer, for initiating me into the world of Facebook.

Thanks to my dear friend Teresa Mitchell, CEO of Great Lakes Seaway Trail Discovery Center. She was the first to suggest that I should write a book. Without her encouragement, this book would still be a collection of sketches and notes. Her gentle prodding put this book in motion.

I also would like to recognize the museums and the art centers that have asked me to lecture and demonstrate my work, allowing me to address a large number of people in a narrow time frame and encourage them to think outside of the box:

- Great Lakes Seaway Trail Discovery Center
- Traditional Arts in Upstate New York
- Hamilton Center for the Arts
- Frederic Remington Art Museum
- Jefferson County Historical Society (New York)
- View art center (Old Forge, New York)

I initiated contact with C&T Publishing because I liked the quality and style of its work. Little did I realize the wonderful editorial staff I would be working with; my editors, Lynn Koolish, Janice Wray, and Ann Haley answered my many questions and helped me to present my work in the required style.

✳ NOTE

My first step in selecting and designing the blocks in this book was to check for usable designs and the dates they were first created. I wanted blocks that were in the public domain, blocks that were tried and true. I have used artistic license in naming the blocks because in many cases the same name was used for different designs. My source for this information was Barbara Brackman's *Encyclopedia of Pieced Quilt Patterns* (Paducah, Kentucky: American Quilter's Society, 1993).

INTRODUCTION

No Line on the Horizon, 76" × 93", 2010

The quilt uses purple with cool undertones. The individual blocks are 15" × 15", made from fabric that I hand dyed in small batches. The quilt is machine pieced and quilted. Blocks: Rolling (page 42), Starlight (page 27), Corner Half (page 43), 1922 (page 26), Fan (page 23), Whirl (page 53), Snow Crystals (page 30), Butte (page 59), Carp (page 32), Moth (page 51), Feathers (page 47), and Enigma (page 52).

My first exposure to drawing a block was not a very precise project. This first venture into design was in 1982. I had small, 2½" × 2½" sketches that I enlarged on a copy machine until they were 8" × 8". To say that they were distorted would be an understatement. I made 20 blocks based on the 8-point star design. I was sure that they would be perfect upon completion because I used a red ballpoint ink pen to mark the seam allowances! The blocks were trued up by the addition of a black framing strip. This quilt, named *Pink and Blue Stars*, was used by one of my sons for the next 25 years—it is still one of my favorites.

I remedied the above experience by developing a simple and accurate way to make those blocks and many more. In this book, I present

☐ easy-to-create blocks for you to make in any size,

☐ no mathematical calculations, and

☐ drawing lines that are clear and easy to follow.

This book is addressed to quilters and other artisans who enjoy the process as much as the finished product. This is the reason why many of us enjoy traveling to new places. We want to create and experience something different than what our friends and neighbors have done.

I think design, fabric, and quality workmanship are critical to making an enjoyable, lasting piece of work. I like to draft my patterns using sound mathematical proportions so that the quilt will be pleasing to the eye. The fabric must be top quality in drape and

colorfastness. I want my quilts to be in use longer than I am, so the workmanship must be top-notch; but I also want them to have a "look at me, touch me" appeal.

I prefer designing in black and white. All of my initial work is done in pencil with an occasional red, blue, or green dot to mark construction points. This keeps the design process simple. Once the design is done, light, medium, and dark values can be used to individualize the project. The end result is a quilt of glorious color.

When I first started quilting, I thought that a quilt should be made to cover a bed. I soon learned that quilts can be wonderful pieces of wall art. I now make a few bed quilts a year and several pieces of wall art. I try to make a hand-quilted, queen-size bed quilt every two years as well as several machine-quilted bed quilts for my family.

Over the course of my career, I have worked with combinations of math and art club students and their teachers to expand their fields into the world of quilts. I used simple tools to show them how to create complex designs based on circles and stars. They were able to design original, accurate eight-point star designs quickly and easily. They also constructed designs based on the division of a circle into five parts and into six parts. They were amazed that these divisions yielded so many design components to work with.

With the above thoughts in mind, let's move on so you can create your own designs—there is nothing more rewarding than making an original piece of your own.

GETTING STARTED

Raising Sand, 75" × 92", 2010

The quilt uses purple with warm undertones. The individual blocks are 15" × 15". Many of the fabrics used in this quilt came from a single packet of fat quarters. The quilt is machine pieced and quilted. Blocks: Castle Wall (page 57), Even (page 60), Spy (page 55), Basic Two-Point Stand (page 17), Fish (page 40), Swallows (page 19), Onstar (page 18), Basic One-Point Stand (page 49), Bat (page 24), Peony (page 25), Double Star (page 50), and Forbidden Fruit (page 61).

 If I had to choose descriptive terms for this book, I would use *intriguing*, *versatile*, and *flexible*, adding that it's great for beginners as well as experienced quilters.

This book will allow you to create your own original quilt with blocks in the size of your choice—your designs can be a small sampler of 8" blocks or a mural large enough to grace the side of a barn.

If I said, "Make a Nine-Patch block that is 6" × 6"," most quilters would have no problem. You could use ordinary graph paper. If I next asked you to "make a Nine-Patch block that is 8" × 8"," I would sense a revolt brewing.

The mathematician in me wants to present information in a bulleted hierarchy. The artist in me wants to be creative and hold your attention. The science teacher in me wants to provide you with usable information. My mind works in the same order when designing a project. All of these qualifiers come into play each step of the way.

My quilts are a meld of many aspects of my background. I enjoy the process of designing and combining. I love that "How'd she do it?" look on a viewer's face. And then the teacher in me enjoys explaining just how I did it. Many of my quilts show the influence of my training in the life sciences. I taught biology to high school students for many years. Then as now, creating interest in a field requires input from many related areas. I enjoy combining the preciseness of mathematical measurement with the excitement of fabric and the art of nature.

This book includes instructions on using a grid-based method to draft 35 blocks—you choose the size you want to use. This way you can easily and accurately create quilts that are uniquely yours.

Refer to the sections on template making and sewing techniques as needed. The fabric choices and the dimensions of a quilt are unique to each quilter—this book provides creative, accurate, and efficient ways to design, cut, and piece.

This book originally started out as a technique book. The quilts that I made to illustrate it are so varied that I felt it important to include several projects to get you started using your blocks. Each of the projects highlights a few special considerations. Be sure to read through each one for the details.

Tools

I have a few favorite tools that I must have for drawing:

- Paper tape
- Mechanical pencil
- Eraser
- Compass
- Dividers or calipers
- Straight edge (such as a ruler)
- Protractor

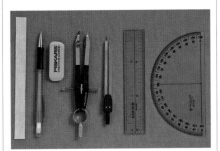

Drawing tools

Yes, a "paper tape," a piece of paper that you use for measuring. Did I mention that the tools I use are inexpensive? The use of all of these tools is explained in How to Draw the Blocks (pages 12–15). You will also need a ruler for a few tasks.

For machine piecing and quilting, I use:

- A stiletto and pincer snips
- A Bernina 550 QE machine, using the Bernina stitch regulator (BSR) when doing free-motion quilting
- A 15" wooden hoop, #12 needles, a Hera marker or chalk, and silk thread for hand quilting

Warm-Up Exercise

I've chosen two basic designs to get you into the swing of things. I refer to them as Basic One-Point Stand and Basic Two-Point Stand. I know that they have many official-sounding names, but this seemed to be the clearest description as the first star is actually standing on one point and the second is standing on two points. In fact, with regard to names of some of the many stars in this book, you'll notice that I've taken creative license and named them as I see fit. Feel free to do the same with your own sketches.

The following directions are for making rough sketches so you can see how easy the process is. If you are in a creative mood while waiting for an appointment, try this using a subscription card insert found in a magazine. They make a perfect paper tape and a straightedge. But any piece of stiff paper that has a straight edge will work as a paper tape.

3. Draw light lines connecting **1** to **4**, **2** to **7**, **3** to **6**, and **5** to **8**.

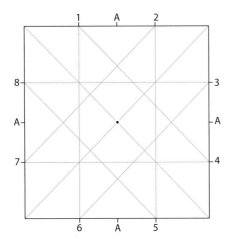

4. Use the intersecting lines to draw the Basic Two-Point Stand star (shown in blue). Don't forget to draw in the spokes (shown in red) to complete the 8-diamond center. Erase the light lines drawn in Steps 1, 2, and 3.

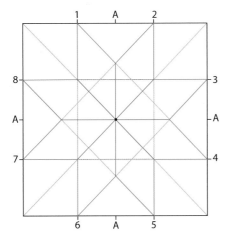

Basic Two-Point Stand star

Below are two advanced quilts based on the blocks in the warm-up exercise. Look at how the basic blocks that you drew in the exercise can be developed into the more advanced designs.

Forbidden Fruit

Peony

THE GRID

 The blocks are drawn on a predrawn grid. It's important to understand that the grid used in this process is not just a series of random-sized boxes placed in a square. The interior squares are carefully planned so the various inner shapes (diamonds, kites, squares, triangles, and—dare I say—trapezoids), will have equal proportions.

One of the nice things about this grid is that it changes proportionately as you change the size of your basic block. That basic finished block size is the only numerical reference you need in this entire process. Yep, that's right, *no mathematical calculations*. Did you notice that I do not have a calculator on my list of tools? You really don't even need a ruler except to mark the size of the outer edge of your block. What you use is a clean master grid that can be covered with tracing paper and used again and again.

This book includes full-size grids in several sizes ready for you to use (pattern pullout pages P3–P4). These grids are in 8″ × 8″, 12″ × 12″, 15″ × 15″, and 18″ × 18″ sizes. If you prefer to draft your own master grid, see Create Your Own Grid (page 108).

On this page are small grids for a block that fits on a page of this book, so you can see how they work. The first grid (above right) is marked in squares, and this is the one I use in this book. The second grid (below right) is marked with colored reference points. Every now and then I have a student who finds that there are just too many lines to follow on the squares grid, so I have included this as an alternative. They both result in the same end product, so choose the one that is easier for you to follow.

When using any grid, the master should be kept intact and clean. Overlay the master grid with tracing paper when you are drafting blocks. Secure the tracing paper with low tack tape.

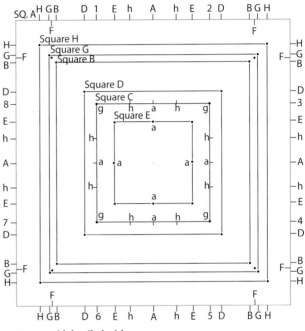

Master grid detailed with squares

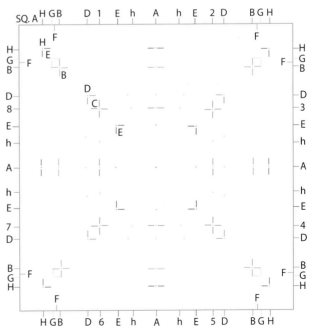

Master grid detailed with reference points

HOW TO DRAW THE BLOCKS

General Directions for Drawing Individual Blocks

 When you begin a project, decide what size to make the blocks—use one of the grids provided (pattern pullout pages P3–P4) or draw one of your own (Create Your Own Grid, page 108). And of course, decide which blocks you would like to make.

As you learned in the warm-up exercise (page 7), reference squares are used to draft the individual block designs. These squares are labeled on the master grid **A**, **H**, **G**, **B**, **D**, **C**, and **E**. Read through the instructions for your chosen block (pages 16–63) and note which of the reference squares you will need to help you draw that block.

All of the specifics for drawing the blocks are included with each block design in the next chapter (The Blocks, pages 16–63), but the general process is as follows.

1. Place the tracing paper over the master grid and secure in place with low-tack tape, such as painters tape or drafting tape. Trace around the outer **Square A**. Mark the center of the block and the **A** and the **1**, **2**, **3**, **4**, **5**, **6**, **7**, and **8** points around the outside edge. Mark any other reference squares and points as directed for each block.

> ☀ **NOTE**
>
> If you want to jump right in to complete a project, 24 blocks have been drafted for you. Templates for traditional piecing or paper-guided piecing are provided on the pullout (pages P1-P2).

2. Start in the center of the block. Lightly draw short horizontal, vertical, and diagonal spokes that radiate from the center. Do this by lining up the path from the center of the master grid to the centers (A) and the outer corners. Unless the instructions specify how long to draw the spokes, start by making them approximately ¼ the width of the block you are drawing. They will be adjusted later, as your block comes together.

3. Next, work at the outer edge of the block. Refer to the number and letter guides to line up a straightedge along the proper path as you did in the warm-up exercise. Most of the lines are made by lining up numbers or letters and drawing a line to connect them, while leaving breaks (or spaces) between specified reference points along the path. These alignments are usually made horizontally, vertically, or diagonally across the block. Watch for the reference points along this alignment and note that many of the breaks are at horizontal, vertical, and diagonal centers.

4. Continue lining up and joining any additional guides, again breaking drawn lines at reference points.

5. Finish extending and connecting any remaining areas, and then erase any unneeded lines.

Now that you have reviewed the general instructions, do you notice anything missing? Math! Mathematical calculations are not used, nor will they be used on any of the following design pages. Another tool that I hope you will depend on only slightly will be an eraser. Make fine lines. Colored pencils are also helpful. If you follow the directions, there should be few extraneous lines.

Terms

The following terms are important for this book.

▪ **Accuracy**

Exactness is essential. Use a pencil with a fine, sharp point because even a fat pencil line can throw off dimensions. Use dividers or calipers to check spaces for exactness.

▪ **Paper tape**

This is a one-time-use tool. Cut a strip of paper about 1″ longer than the distance you wish to measure. Put tick marks on the strip to denote the distance you are measuring. Use it like a ruler.

▪ **Straightedge**

Used to draw straight lines, a straightedge can be a ruler, but it doesn't need to be. It can be a thin piece of plastic with a beveled edge.

▪ **Long diagonal**

This line or measurement goes from one corner to the opposite corner of a block.

▪ **Short or corner diagonal**

This is a line drawn from a number to a number across the corner of a block.

Tricks of the Trade

The following techniques are simple ways for achieving accuracy in the designs in this book as well as in many other patterns you may work with.

MAKING SURE YOUR SQUARE IS REALLY SQUARE

This is the crucial first step in designing a block that is accurate and pleasing to the eye. First check using a protractor, and then confirm using the paper tape as described below.

Use a Protractor

1. Put the crosshairs of the protractor exactly on the corner of the square.

2. The 90° line should be exactly on the square's vertical line.

3. The 0° line should be exactly on the square's horizontal line.

4. Check each corner and adjust if necessary.

Use a Paper Tape—Method 1

1. Measure each long diagonal of the square to be sure that they are exactly the same.

2. If the diagonals are not the same, then measure the sides to see which sides match the desired measurement and which sides should be adjusted.

Use a Paper Tape—Method 2

1. Align a paper tape along a side of the square and use tick marks to indicate the length.

2. Measure the other 3 sides with the paper tape, to see if all sides are the same length.

3. Adjust if necessary.

4. Repeat Steps 2 and 3 if you make adjustments.

DIVIDING A LINE EXACTLY IN HALF

This is my preferred method for finding the midpoint on any line because the results are so accurate. There are other ways, but I find them to be less accurate. When these inaccuracies are multiplied within a block, it can cause problems.

1. Use a straightedge to draw a straight, horizontal line about ½" longer than the actual line you want to divide. Mark the exact length of the line you want to divide onto a piece of paper tape.

2. Mark a blue dot about ¼" in from the left edge of the drawn line. Use the paper tape to measure and mark a red dot on the drawn line at the end of the measurement. Note: The slight excess at each end of the line helps with accurate placement of the measurement.

3. Place the point of a compass into the blue dot. Adjust the compass so that the pencil end is just past the approximate center of the line. Swing an arc. Lift but do not adjust the compass, and place the compass point on the red dot. Draw another arc that intersects the first arc.

4. Draw a line joining the points where the arcs cross. This line divides the measured length in half.

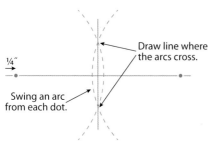

Divide line exactly in half.

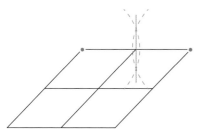

Use same technique to divide each side of a diamond, to divide the diamond equally.

FINDING THE CENTER POINT OF A DIAMOND

1. Draw a vertical line from point to point inside the diamond.

2. Draw a horizontal line from point to point inside the diamond.

3. Mark the center point where the 2 lines cross.

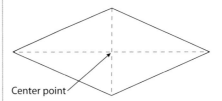

Center point

Finding center of diamond

DIVIDING A LINE INTO THIRDS

This is one instance where you will need to use a ruler.

1. Draw a straight, horizontal line about ½" longer than the actual line you want to divide.

2. Use a paper tape to note the actual length of the line you want to divide. Mark a blue dot about ¼" in from the left edge of the drawn line. Using the paper tape, mark a red dot on the line at the end of the measurement. Note: The slight excess at each end of the line helps with accurate placement of the measurement.

3. Draw perpendicular lines at each end of the actual measure by placing the crosshairs of a protractor on the blue and red dots and making a short 90° line straight up.

4. Place the zero mark of a ruler exactly on the blue dot. Angle the ruler across the measured line at a slight elevation until it aligns with the upright with the red dot at the base with a measurement that is easily divisible by 3, such as 4½.

5. Divide the measurement from Step 4 by 3 and mark green dots at the one-third intervals on the rule. For example, if the number from Step 4 is 4½, mark green dots at the 1½ and 3 markings on the ruler.

6. Use a protractor to line up the green dots down to the baseline. Draw perpendicular lines down to the baseline (shown in red). These lines divide the measure length into thirds.7.

7. Finally, use dividers or a compass to make sure each division of the line is exactly the same.

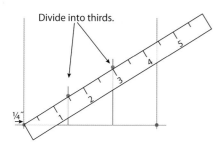

Dividing line into three equal sections

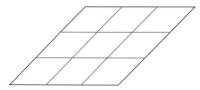

Use this technique to equally divide each side of the diamond, and then connect the marks.

SUBDIVIDING SQUARE C

This is the easiest and most accurate way to get the small triangles, squares, and diamonds that are used in some of the blocks in this book, such as Swallows (page 19), Facets (page 20), and Fish (page 40), and in other blocks that you might create yourself. For example, when you are making 8″ × 8″ blocks and want to place small diamonds within the diamond shapes of the 8″ × 8″ block, just follow the steps below to create the small diamonds exactly the right size. When you use the following method, these components will increase and decrease in proportion to the block size.

1. Refer to Basic Two-Point Stand Star (page 9) and Create Your Own Grid (page 108) to reproduce **Square C** accurately, or trace over your master grid.

2. Draft a Basic Two-Point Stand star *inside* **Square C** (page 17).

3. Make freezer-paper templates (page 65) of the resulting square, diamond, and triangle, and use them in designs such as Swallows, Facets, and Fish.

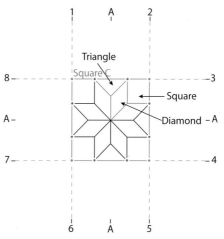

Square C subdivided inside larger block

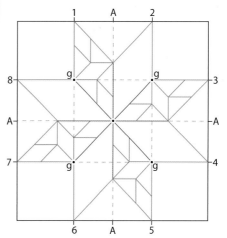

Facets block using subdivided Square C triangle and diamond.

The Blocks

BASIC TWO-POINT STAND

1. Select the grid for your chosen block size, using the 8", 12", 15", or 18" master grids on pullout pages P3–P4 or draw your own grid (page 108). Overlay a sheet of tracing paper and trace the outside **Square A**, markings **1 to 8**, and the **A** centers. Referring to **Square C**, mark the **g** points. Lightly draw in the horizontal and vertical centerlines.

2. Start by drawing the spokes of the center diamonds (shown in gray) in the center of the block: Line up the path across the center and draw diagonal lines connecting the **g** points. Draw vertical and horizontal lines across the center, about the same length as the diagonal lines—they will be adjusted later.

3. Next work around the outer edge of the block. Refer to the numbers and letters on the master grid to line up a straightedge along the proper path, breaking the lines between the points indicated (shown in blue).

   a. Line up and draw vertical lines from **1** to **6** and **2** to **5**, breaking between **g** points.

   b. Line up and draw horizontal lines from **8** to **3** and **7** to **4**, breaking between **g** points.

4. Line up and draw diagonal lines from **1** to **4**, **2** to **7**, **3** to **6**, and **5** to **8**, breaking between the vertical and horizontal centers (shown in red).

5. Complete the spokes of the center diamonds and erase any unnecessary guide lines.

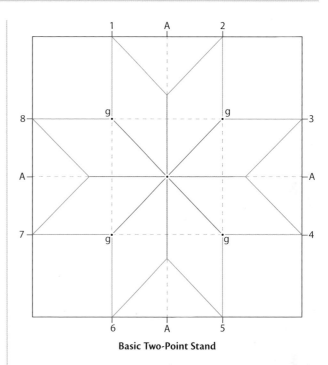

Basic Two-Point Stand

ONSTAR

1. Select the grid for your chosen block size using the 8", 12", 15", or 18" master grids on pullout pages P3–P4 or draw your own grid (page 108). Overlay a sheet of tracing paper and trace the outside **Square A**, markings **1** to **8**, and the **A** centers. Referring to **Square C**, mark the **g** points. Lightly draw in the horizontal and vertical centerlines.

2. Repeat Steps 2–5 for the Basic Two-Point Stand star (page 17). This star is now shown in gray and blue.

3. Divide the diamonds.

a. Find the center point of each diamond (page 14), and mark with a dot.

b. Line up the center points of diamonds diagonally across from each other (diamonds **1** to **4**, **2** to **7**, **3** to **6**, and **5** to **8**), and draw a dividing line inside each diamond (shown in red).

c. Line up the center points of diamonds vertically across from each other (diamonds **1** to **6** and **2** to **5**), and draw a dividing line inside each diamond (shown in green). Repeat horizontally (from diamonds **3** to **8** and **4** to **7**).

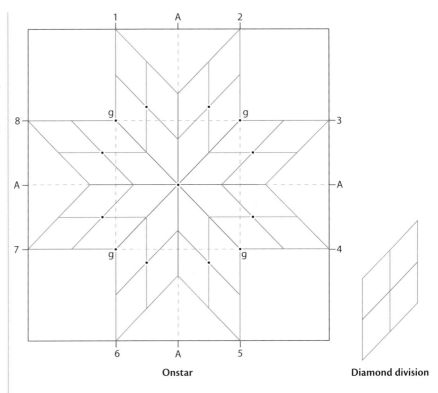

Onstar

Diamond division

SWALLOWS

1. Select the grid for your chosen block size using the 8″, 12″, 15″, or 18″ master grids on pullout pages P3–P4 or draw your own grid (page 108). Overlay a sheet of tracing paper and trace the outside **Square A**, markings **1** to **8**, and the **A** centers. Referring to **Square C**, mark the **g** points. Lightly draw in the horizontal and vertical centerlines.

2. Repeat Steps 2–5 for the Basic Two-Point Stand star (page 17). This star is now shown in gray and blue.

3. Divide the diamonds.

a. Trace **Square C** on a separate piece of paper. Refer to Subdividing Square C (page 15) to draft a Basic Two-Point Stand star inside the **Square C** of your block.

b. Make freezer-paper templates of the resulting diamond and triangle. Arrange and trace them (shown in red) inside the large diamonds..

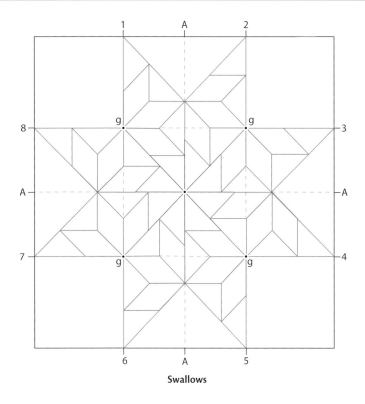

Swallows

FACETS

1. Select the grid for your chosen block size using the 8″, 12″, 15″, or 18″ master grids on pullout pages P3–P4 or draw your own grid (page 108). Overlay a sheet of tracing paper and trace the outside **Square A**, markings **1** to **8**, and the **A** centers. Referring to **Square C**, mark the **g** points. Lightly draw in the horizontal and vertical centerlines.

2. Repeat Steps 2–5 for the Basic Two-Point Stand star (page 17). This star is now shown in gray and blue.

3. Divide the diamonds.

a. Refer to Subdividing Square C (page 15) to draft a Basic Two-Point Stand star inside the **Square C** of your block.

b. Make freezer-paper templates of the resulting diamond and triangle. Arrange and trace them (shown in red) inside 4 alternating large diamonds.

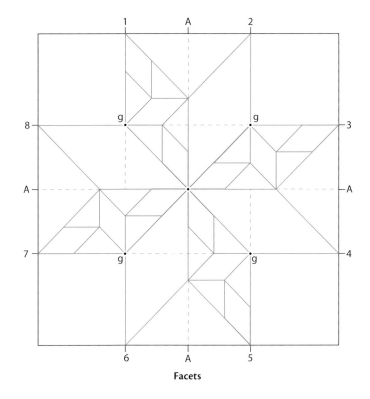

Facets

TWO-POINT-ONE

1. Select the grid for your chosen block size using the 8″, 12″, 15″, or 18″ master grids on pullout pages P3–P4 or draw your own grid (page 108). Overlay a sheet of tracing paper and trace the outside **Square A**, markings **1** to **8**, and the **A** centers. Referring to **Square E**, **Square D**, and **Square B**, mark the **E**, **D**, and **B** points. Lightly draw in the horizontal and vertical centerlines.

2. First work around the outer edge of the block. Refer to the numbers and letters on the master grid to line up a straightedge along the proper path, breaking the lines between the points indicated.

   a. Line up and draw short diagonal lines across each corner through the **B** points, from **2** to **3**, **4** to **5**, **6** to **7**, and **8** to **1** (shown in gray).

   b. Line up **A** with an opposite **B** point, going through **E**, and draw a line from **A** to **B**, breaking in the center area between the **E** point and the **D** line. Repeat all around the block (shown in blue).

3. Draw the center motif.

   a. Line up and draw the center square by connecting the **E** points.

   b. Draft a Basic Two-Point Stand star (page 9) inside this square (shown in red).

4. Erase any unnecessary guide lines.

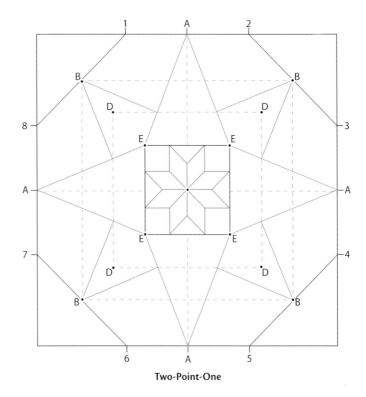

Two-Point-One

BALL

1. Select the grid for your chosen block size using the 8″, 12″, 15″, or 18″ master grids on pullout pages P3–P4 or draw your own grid (page 108). Overlay a sheet of tracing paper and trace the outside **Square A**, markings **1** to **8**, **h points**, and the **A** centers. Referring to **Square C**, mark the **g** points. Mark the **h** points on the outside edge. Lightly draw in the horizontal and vertical centerlines.

2. Start in the center of the block by drawing the spokes of the center kites (shown in gray). First align a straightedge vertically and horizontally through the outside edge **h** points and place dots where they intersect; name them all **h**. Line up the path across the center and draw diagonal lines connecting the new **h** points.

3. Next work around the outer edge of the block. Refer to the numbers and letters on the master grid to line up a straightedge along the proper path, breaking the lines between the points indicated (shown in blue).

   a. Line up and draw vertical lines from **1** to **6** and **2** to **5**, breaking between **g** points.

   b. Line up and draw horizontal lines from **8** to **3** and **7** to **4**, breaking between **g** points.

   c. Line up and draw diagonal lines from **1** to **4**, **2** to **7**, **3** to **6**, and **5** to **8**, breaking between the vertical and horizontal centers.

4. To form the long points of the kites that encircle the center, draw lines to connect 2 **h** dots to the inner corner of a large triangle. Repeat around the block (shown in red).

5. To form the 4 diamonds that encircle the center, draw lines connecting the **g** points to the long kite points. Repeat around the block (shown in green).

6. Erase any unnecessary lines.

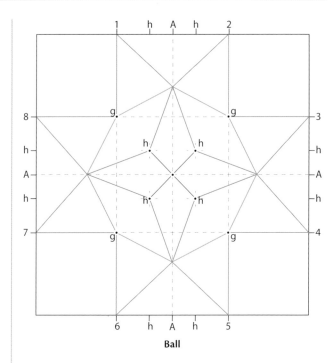

Ball

The photo at the top of this page is a a variation of this block created by rotating the center star.

FAN

1. Select the grid for your chosen block size using the 8″, 12″, 15″, or 18″ master grids on pullout pages P3–P4 or draw your own grid (page 108). Overlay a sheet of tracing paper and trace the outside **Square A**, markings **1** to **8**, and the **A** centers. Referring to **Square C**, mark the **g** and **h** points. Lightly draw in the horizontal and vertical centerlines.

2. Start by drawing the spokes of the center diamonds (shown in gray) in the center of the block: Line up the path across the center and draw diagonal lines connecting the **g** points. Draw vertical and horizontal lines across the center, about the same length as the diagonal lines—they will be adjusted later.

3. Next work around the outer edge of the block. Refer to the numbers and letters on the master grid to line up a straightedge along the proper path, breaking the lines between the points indicated (shown in blue).

   a. Line up and draw vertical lines from **1** to **6** and **2** to **5**, breaking between **h** points.

   b. Line up and draw horizontal lines from **8** to **3** and **7** to **4**, breaking between **h** points.

   c. Line up and draw diagonal lines from **1** to **4**, **2** to **7**, **3** to **6**, and **5** to **8**, breaking between **h** points (shown in blue).

4. To complete the center half-kite shapes, draw lines from **1** to **5**, **2** to **6**, **3** to **7**, and **4** to **8** (shown in red).

5. Complete the spokes of the center diamonds and erase any unnecessary guide lines.

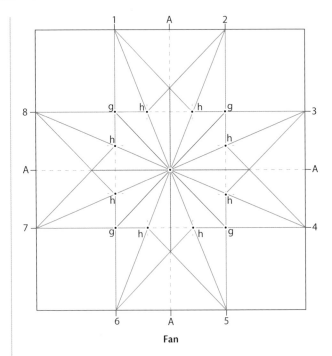

Fan

1922

1. Select the grid for your chosen block size using the 8", 12", 15", or 18" master grids on pullout pages P3–P4 or draw your own grid (page 108). Overlay a sheet of tracing paper and trace the outside **Square A**, markings **1** to **8**, and the **A** centers. Referring to **Square C** and **Square B**, mark the **B**, **g**, and **h** points.

2. First work around the outer edge of the block. Refer to the numbers and letters on the master grid to line up a straightedge along the proper path, breaking the lines between the points indicated (shown in gray).

   a. Line up and draw short diagonal lines across each corner, through the **B** points, from **2** to **3**, **4** to **5**, **6** to **7**, and **8** to **1**.

   b. Line up and draw diagonal lines from **1** to **5**, **2** to **6**, **3** to **7**, and **4** to **8**, breaking in the center area between **h** points.

3. Start the center rectangles (shown in blue).

   a. Line up a straightedge from **1** to **4** and draw a short line in the center from **h** to **h**.

   b. Repeat with **8** to **5**, **2** to **7**, and **3** to **6**.

4. Start the kites (shown in red). Line up an **A** point with an opposite **g** point, across the block, and draw a line from **A** to the first **h** point. Repeat all around the block.

Note that the sides of the elongated triangles on either side of the red kite tails are not equal but the sides of the kite shapes are equal.

5. Complete the center motif (shown in green).

   a. Line up diagonally across the center and draw a line from points **h** to **h**.

   b. Repeat all around to complete a center square surrounded by 4 rectangles.

6. Erase any unnecessary guide lines.

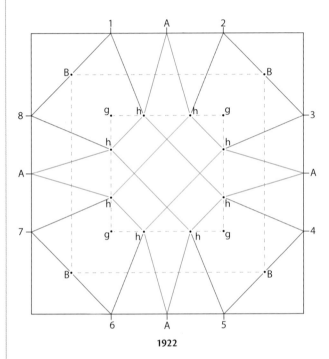

1922

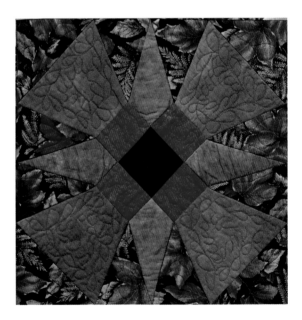

4. Work with reference point **D** to draw corner diamonds (shown in red).

a. Line up long diagonals from corner to opposite corner. Draw short lines from point **B** to point **D** in each corner.

b. Line up outer marks **D** to **D** vertically. Draw a short line through point **D**, extending in *each direction* about the same distance as **B** to **D**.

c. Line up outer marks **D** to **D** horizontally. Draw a short line through point **D**, extending in *each direction* about the same distance as **B** to **D**.

5. Complete the corner diamonds and inner on-point squares (shown in green).

a. Line up an outer **B** marking in the upper left corner diagonally across to an outer **B** marking in the lower right corner. Draw a line connecting the outer **B** markings, first breaking between the extended **D** lines from Step 4b, then breaking in the center area between the **E** lines and again between the next set of extended **D** lines. Repeat around the block.

b. Line up an outer **E** marking in the upper left corner diagonally across to an outer **E** marking in the lower right corner. Draw a line from the vertical centerline to the horizontal centerline (where they meet **Square B**), breaking in the center area between the **D** lines. Repeat around the block to finish the on-point squares. Mark the corners of the on-point squares with yellow dots to be used as reference points in Step 6..

c. Draw diagonal lines across the corners from outer markings **E** to **E**, breaking in the center area between the extended **D** lines from Step 4b. Repeat around the block.

6. To complete the remaining 4 squares and the center diamonds, line up the yellow dots made in Step 5b. Draw vertical and horizontal lines from dot to dot, breaking where it meets the center spokes from Step 2.

7. Erase any unnecessary guide lines and adjust the spokes.

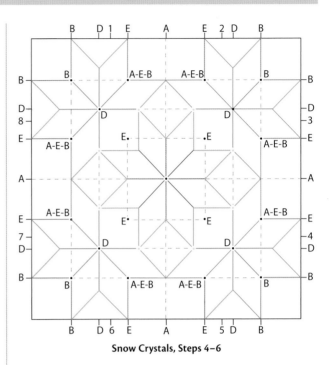

Snow Crystals, Steps 4–6

CARP

1. Select the grid for your chosen block size using the 8″, 12″, 15″, or 18″ master grids on pullout pages P3–P4 or draw your own grid (page 108). Overlay a sheet of tracing paper and trace the outside **Square A**, markings **1** to **8**, outer marks **B** and **E**, and the **A** centers. Referring to **Square E**, **Square D**, and **Square B**, mark the **E**, **D**, and **B** points. Lightly draw in the horizontal and vertical centerlines.

2. Start by drawing the spokes of the center diamonds (shown in gray) in the center of the block: Line up the path across the center and draw vertical and horizontal lines between the **E** lines. Draw diagonal lines across the center, about the same length as the vertical and horizontal lines—these will be adjusted later.

3. Next work around the outer edge of the block. Refer to the numbers and letters on the master grid to line up a straightedge along the proper path, breaking the lines between the points indicated (shown in gray).

   a. Line up and draw vertical lines from **1** to **6** and **2** to **5**, breaking in the center area between the **B** lines on the master grid.

   b. Line up and draw horizontal lines from **8** to **3** and **7** to **4**, breaking in the center area between **B** lines.

   c. Line up and draw vertical lines connecting the outer **B** markings, breaking between the lines drawn in Step 3b.

   d. Line up and draw horizontal lines connecting the outer **B** markings, breaking between the lines drawn in Step 3a.

   e. Line up the long diagonals from corner to opposite corner and draw short lines from points **B** to **D** in each corner.

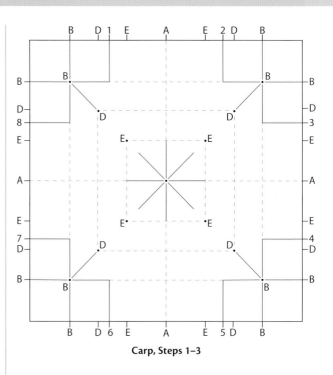

Carp, Steps 1–3

4. Start the ring of outer diamonds (shown in gray).

a. Line up and draw lines from **A** to **A** vertically and horizontally, breaking in the center area between the **B** lines on the master grid.

b. Line up and draw diagonal lines across the corners, from **A** to **A**, breaking in the center area between the **B** lines—these will be adjusted later.

c. Line up **1** to **4** and draw a line, breaking between the diagonal lines drawn in Step 4b. Repeat for **2** to **7**, **3** to **6**, and **5** to **8**. Mark dots at these intersections (shown in red) to be used as reference points in Step 6.

5. Start the inner squares (shown in blue): Line up and draw vertical and horizontal lines from points **D** to **D**, breaking in the center area—these will be adjusted later.

6. Complete the horizontal and vertical sides of the inner squares (shown in red).

a. Vertically line up the reference points made in Step 4c, and draw lines from point to point, breaking in the center area between the center spokes.

b. Horizontally line up the reference points made in Step 4c, and draw lines from point to point, breaking in the center area between the center spokes.

7. Complete the diamonds and squares (shown in green).

a. Line up an outer **B** marking in the upper left corner diagonally across to an outer **B** marking in the lower right corner. Draw a line between the **B** lines on the master grid, breaking in the center area between the **E** lines. Repeat all around the block.

b. Line up an outer **E** marking in the upper left corner diagonally across to an outer **E** marking in the lower right corner. Draw a line between the **B** lines on the master grid, breaking in the center area between the **D** lines. Repeat all around the block.

8. Finish extending and connecting lines to complete the block, and erase any unnecessary guide lines.

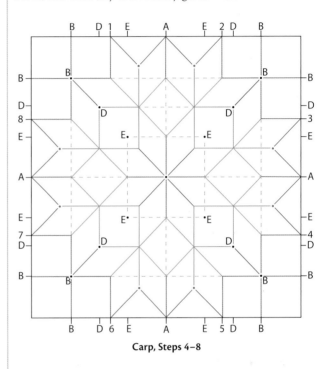

Carp, Steps 4–8

KITE TAILS

1. Select the grid for your chosen block size using the 8″, 12″, 15″, or 18″ master grids on pullout pages P3–P4 or draw your own grid (page 108). Overlay a sheet of tracing paper and trace the outside **Square A**, outer markings **1** to **8**, **B** and the **A** centers. Referring to **Square E**, **Square D**, and **Square B**, mark the **E**, **D**, and **B** points. Lightly draw in the horizontal and vertical centerlines and the long diagonals.

2. Start by drawing the spokes of the center diamonds (shown in gray) in the center of the block: Line up the path across the center and draw vertical and horizontal lines between the **E** lines. Draw diagonal lines across the center, about the same length as the vertical and horizontal lines—these will be adjusted later.

3. Next work around the outer edge of the block. Refer to the numbers and letters on the master grid to line up a straightedge along the proper path, breaking the lines between the points indicated.

a. Line up **A** with an opposite **B** point and draw a line from **A** through point **B**, extending to the outer edge and breaking in the center area between the **D** lines. Repeat around the block (shown in blue). Mark dots on the **D** lines where these lines meet each other, to be used later as reference points.

b. Line up an outer **B** marking in the upper left corner diagonally across to an outer **B** marking in the lower right corner. Draw a line between the **D** lines on the master grid, breaking in the center area between the horizontal and vertical centers (where the new line meets the **E** lines). Repeat around the block (shown in green).

c. Vertically line up the reference points made in Step 3a, and draw lines from point to point (shown in red), breaking in the center area between the center spokes (or the long diagonal lines).

d. Horizontally line up the reference points made in Step 3a, and draw lines from point to point (shown in red), breaking in the center area between the center spokes (or the long diagonal lines).

4. Complete the spokes of the center kites, and erase any unnecessary guide lines.

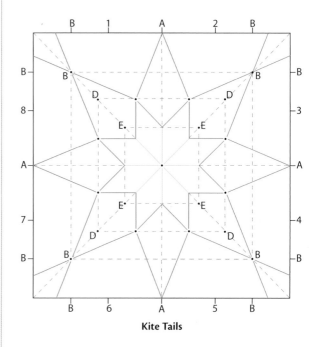

Kite Tails

THREE RINGS

1. Select the grid for your chosen block size using the 8", 12", 15", or 18" master grids on pullout pages P3–P4 or draw your own grid (page 108). Overlay a sheet of tracing paper and trace the outside **Square A**, markings **1** to **8**, and the **A** centers. Referring to **Square E**, **Square D**, and **Square B**, mark the **E**, **D**, and **B** points. Lightly draw in the horizontal and vertical centerlines, **Square D** and the long diagonals.

2. Start by drawing the spokes of the center diamonds (shown in gray in the center of the block): Line up the path across the center and draw vertical and horizontal lines between the **E** lines. Draw diagonal lines across the center, about the same length as the vertical and horizontal lines—these will be adjusted later.

3. Next work around the outer edge of the block. Refer to the numbers and letters on the master grid to line up a straightedge along the proper path, breaking the lines between the points indicated (shown in gray).

a. Draw short diagonal lines across each corner through the **B** points, from **2** to **3**, **4** to **5**, **6** to **7**, and **8** to **1**.

b. Draw **Square B**. Mark dots where the **B** lines cross the lightly drawn horizontal and vertical center guide lines.

c. Draw diagonal lines across the corners from **A** to **A** through point **D**.

4. Start the inner squares.

a. Line up a vertical center on a **B** line with a horizontal center on a **B** line and draw a diagonal line breaking in the center area between the **D** lines. Repeat all around the block (shown in red). Mark dots where these diagonals touch the **D** lines, to be used later as reference points.

b. Draw vertical lines from **D** to **D** (shown in blue), breaking in the center area between the points marked in Step 4a.

c. Draw horizontal lines from **D** to **D** (shown in blue), breaking in the center area between the points marked in Step 4a.

5. Complete the squares (shown in green).

a. Vertically line up the reference points made in Step 4a, and draw lines from point to point, breaking in the center area between the center spokes (or the lightly drawn long diagonal lines).

b. Horizontally line up the reference points made in Step 4a, and draw lines from point to point, breaking in the center area between the center spokes (or the lightly drawn long diagonal lines).

c. Diagonally line up the reference points made in Step 4a and draw lines from point to point, breaking in the center of the **Square E** lines.

6. Complete the spokes of the center kites, and erase any unnecessary guide lines.

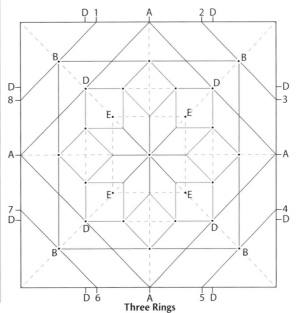

Three Rings

MAGICAL

1. Select the grid for your chosen block size using the 8″, 12″, 15″, or 18″ master grids on pullout pages P3–P4 or draw your own grid (page 108). Overlay a sheet of tracing paper and trace the outside **Square A**, markings **1** to **8**, **B** and the **A** centers. Referring to **Square E**, **Square D**, and **Square B**, mark the **E**, **D**, and **B** points. Lightly draw in the horizontal and vertical centerlines and the long diagonals.

2. Start by drawing the spokes of the center diamonds (shown in gray in the center of the block): Line up the path across the center and draw vertical and horizontal lines between the **E** lines. Draw diagonal lines across the center, about the same length as the vertical and horizontal lines—these will be adjusted later.

3. Next work around the outer edge of the block. Refer to the numbers and letters on the master grid to line up a straightedge along the proper path, breaking the lines between the points indicated (shown in gray).

a. Line up and draw diagonal lines across each corner from **2** to **3**, **4** to **5**, **6** to **7**, and **8** to **1**, passing through the **B** points.

b. Line up and draw vertical lines from **1** to **6** and **2** to **5**, and horizontal lines from **8** to **3** and **7** to **4**, breaking in the large center area between the **B** lines on the master grid.

c. Line up and draw vertical and horizontal lines from **B** to **B** points, breaking in the center area where the lines drawn in Step 3b touch the **B** lines.

4. Draw the edge triangles (shown in gray).

a. Line up and draw diagonal lines across the corners from **A** to **A**, breaking in the center area between the **B** lines—these will be adjusted later.

b. Line up and draw diagonal lines from **1** to **4**, **2** to **7**, **3** to **6**, and **5** to **8**, breaking in the area between where they meet the diagonal lines drawn in Step 4a. Mark dots at these intersections to be used as reference points, and name them **A-N**.

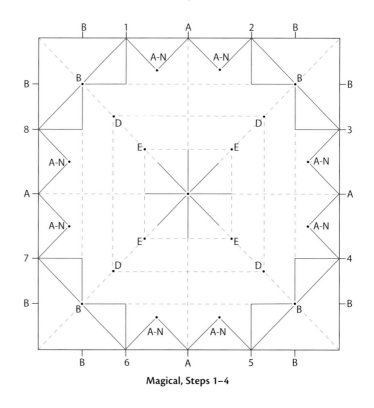

Magical, Steps 1–4

5. Complete the houses.

a. Line up the **A-N** points made in Step 4b and draw vertical lines and horizontal lines (shown in blue) from point to point, breaking in the center area between the center spokes, at the diagonals.

b. Line up from an outer **B** marking in the upper left corner across to an outer **B** marking in the lower right corner, and draw a line from **B** line to **B** line, breaking in the center area between the **E** lines (the center spokes). Repeat around the block (shown in red).

c. Mark a dot where the blue lines from Step 5a intersect with the red lines from Step 5b, to be used as reference points.

6. Complete the inner triangles (shown in green).

a. Line up along the **D** lines vertically and horizontally and draw lines between the reference points from Step 5c.

b. Connect the ends of the lines drawn in Step 6a diagonally all around the block to form an octagon.

7. Adjust the spokes of the center diamonds from Step 2, and erase any unnecessary guide lines.

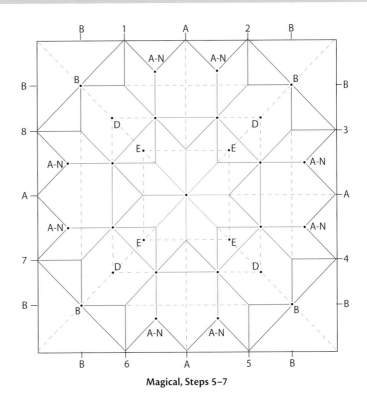

Magical, Steps 5–7

DUTCH ROSE

1. Select the grid for your chosen block size using the 8", 12", 15", or 18" master grids on pullout pages P3–P4 or draw your own grid (page 108). Overlay a sheet of tracing paper and trace the outside **Square A**, markings **1** to **8**, outer **B** marks and the **A** centers. Referring to **Square E**, **Square D**, **Square C**, and **Square B**, mark the **E**, **g**, **D**, and **B** points. Lightly draw in the horizontal and vertical centerlines and the long diagonals.

2. Start by drawing the spokes of the center diamonds (shown in gray) in the center of the block: Line up the path across the center and draw vertical and horizontal lines between the **E** lines. Draw diagonal lines across the center, connecting the **g** points.

3. Next work around the outer edge of the block. Refer to the numbers and letters on the master grid to line up a straightedge along the proper path, breaking the lines between the points indicated (shown in gray).

a. Line up and draw vertical and horizontal lines from **A** to **A**, breaking in the large center area between the **B** lines on the master grid. Mark dots where these lines touch the **B** lines, to be used as reference points, and name them **A-B**.

b. Line up and draw diagonal lines across each corner from **2** to **3**, **4** to **5**, **6** to **7**, and **8** to **1**, passing through the **B** points.

c. Line up and draw vertical lines from **1** to **6** and **2** to **5**, and horizontal lines from **8** to **3** and **7** to **4**, breaking in the center area between the **g** points.

d. Line up and draw vertical and horizontal lines from points **B** to **B**, breaking in the center area where the lines drawn in Step 3c cross the **B** lines.

4. Complete the outer petals (shown in gray).

a. Line up and draw diagonal lines across the corners from **A** to **A**, breaking in the center area between the **B** lines—these will be adjusted in Step 4b.

b. Line up and draw diagonal lines from **1** to **4**, **2** to **7**, **3** to **6**, and **5** to **8**, breaking in the area between where they meet the diagonal lines drawn in Step 4a. Mark dots at these intersections to be used as reference points, and name them **A-N**. Adjust the lines from Step 4a so they end at the **A-N** points.

5. To start the inner petals, line up and draw vertical and horizontal lines (shown in blue) to connect the **A-N** points made in Step 4b, breaking in the center area between the long diagonal lines.

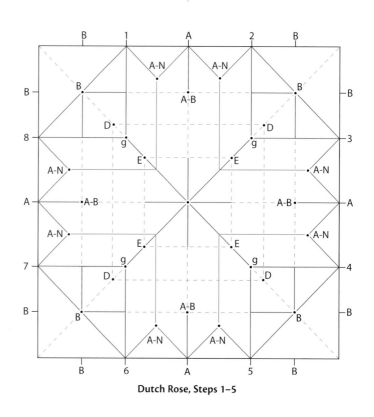

Dutch Rose, Steps 1–5

6. Complete the inner petals.

a. Line up and draw diagonal lines to connect the **A-B** points made in Step 3a, breaking in the center area between the **D** lines (shown in green).

b. Line up from an outer **B** marking in the upper left corner across to an outer **B** marking in the lower right corner and draw a line from **D** line to **D** line, breaking in the center area between the **E** lines (the center spokes). Repeat all around the block (shown in red).

7. Adjust the spokes of the center kites, and erase any unnecessary lines.

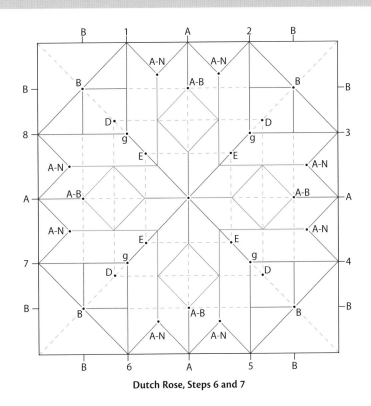

Dutch Rose, Steps 6 and 7

ROLLING

1. Select the grid for your chosen block size using the 8″, 12″, 15″, or 18″ master grids on pullout pages P3–P4 or draw your own grid (page 108). Overlay a sheet of tracing paper and trace the outside **Square A**, markings **1** to **8**, and the **A** centers. Referring to **Square E**, **Square C**, and **Square B**, mark the **E**, **a**, and **B** points. Lightly draw in the horizontal and vertical centerlines and the long diagonals.

2. Start by drawing the spokes of the center diamonds (shown in gray) in the center of the block: Line up the path across the center and draw vertical and horizontal lines between the **a** points. Draw diagonal lines across the center between the **E** points.

3. Next work around the outer edge of the block. Refer to the numbers and letters on the master grid to line up a straightedge along the proper path, breaking the lines between the points indicated (shown in gray).

   a. Line up and draw diagonal lines across each corner from **2** to **3**, **4** to **5**, **6** to **7**, and **8** to **1**, passing through the **B** points.

   b. Line up the **B** points and draw **Square B**.

4. Line up and draw diagonal lines across the corners from **A** to **A**, breaking in the center area between the **B** lines (shown in blue). Mark dots where these lines touch the **B** lines, to be used later as reference points, and name them **B-E**.

5. To make the inner corner squares (shown in red), line up and draw vertical and horizontal lines from points **B-E** to **B-E**, breaking in the center area between the **E** points.

6. Complete the center diamonds (shown in green). Line up and draw diagonal lines from points **B-E** to **B-E**, breaking in the center area between the **a** points. Repeat around the block.

7. Erase any unnecessary guide lines.

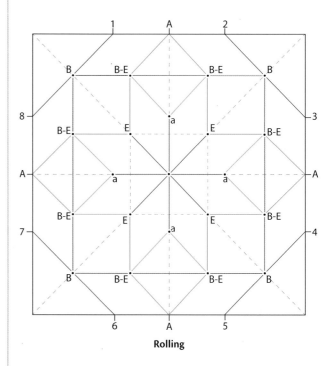

Rolling

CORNER HALF

1. Select the grid for your chosen block size using the 8″, 12″, 15″, or 18″ master grids on pullout pages P3–P4 or draw your own grid (page 108). Overlay a sheet of tracing paper and trace the outside **Square A**, markings **1** to **8**, outer marks **B**, **E**, and the **A** centers. Referring to **Square E**, **Square D**, **Square C**, and **Square B**, mark the **E**, **a**, **D**, and **B** points. Lightly draw in the horizontal and vertical centerlines.

2. Start by drawing the spokes of the center diamonds (shown in gray) in the center of the block: Line up the path across the center and draw vertical and horizontal lines between the **a** points. Draw diagonal lines across the center between the **E** points.

3. Next work around the outer edge of the block. Refer to the numbers and letters on the master grid to line up a straightedge along the proper path, breaking the lines between the points indicated (shown in blue).

   a. Line up and draw vertical and horizontal lines connecting outer markings **E** to **E**, breaking in the center area between the **E** points.

   b. Mark dots on the lines from Step 3a where they cross the **B** lines, to be used later as reference points, and name them **B-E**.

4. Complete the inner triangles (shown in blue).

   a. Line up and draw vertical and horizontal lines from outer markings **B** to **B**, breaking between points **B** and **B-E** and then **B-E** and **B**.

   b. Line up diagonally from outer markings **A** to **A** and draw lines between **B-E** and **B-E**, passing through point **D**. Repeat around the block.

   c. Line up diagonally from the **B-E** marking in the upper left across to the **B-E** marking in the lower right and draw a line, breaking in the center area between the **a** points (the center spokes). Repeat around the block.

Instructions continue on page 44.

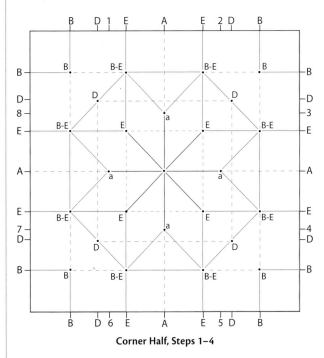

Corner Half, Steps 1–4

5. Start the corner diamonds (shown in red).

a. Line up the long diagonals from corner to corner and draw a short line from **B** to **D** in each corner.

b. Line up vertically and horizontally from **D** to **D**. Draw short lines from points **D** toward the outer edges, about the same length as the **B** to **D** lines.

6. Complete the corner diamonds (shown in green).

a. Line up from an outer **B** marking in the upper left corner across to an outer **B** marking in the lower right corner, and draw short lines from the outer **B** marking toward the center to where the new lines intersect the lines made in Step 5b. Repeat around the block.

b. Line up and draw diagonal lines across the corners from outer mark **E** to outer mark **E**, breaking in the center area where the new lines intersect the lines made in Step 5b.

7. Finish extending and connecting lines to complete the block and erase any unnecessary guide lines.

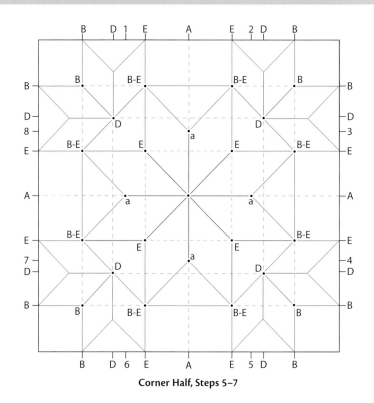

Corner Half, Steps 5–7

RING-A-ROUND

1. Select the grid for your chosen block size using the 8", 12", 15", or 18" master grids on pullout pages P3–P4 or draw your own grid (page 108). Overlay a sheet of tracing paper and trace the outside **Square A**, markings **1** to **8**, and the **A** centers. Referring to **Square E**, **Square C**, and **Square B**, mark the **E**, **a**, and **B** points. Lightly draw in the horizontal and vertical centerlines.

2. Start by drawing the spokes of the center diamonds (shown in gray) in the center of the block: Line up the path across the center and draw vertical and horizontal lines between the **a** points. Draw diagonal lines across the center between the **E** points.

3. Next work around the outer edge of the block. Refer to the numbers and letters on the master grid to line up a straightedge along the proper path, breaking the lines between the points indicated (shown in gray).

a. Line up and draw diagonal lines across each corner from **2** to **3**, **4** to **5**, **6** to **7**, and **8** to **1**, passing through the **B** points.

b. Line up and draw diagonal lines across the corners from **A** to **A**, breaking in the center area between the **B** lines. Mark dots where these lines touch the **B** lines, to be used later

as reference points, and name them **B-E**.

c. Line up and draw vertical and horizontal lines from points **B** to **B**, breaking in the center area between the **B-E** points.

4. To complete the corner squares, line up and draw vertical and horizontal lines from points **B-E** to **B-E** (shown in blue), breaking in the center area between the **E** points.

Instructions continue on page 46.

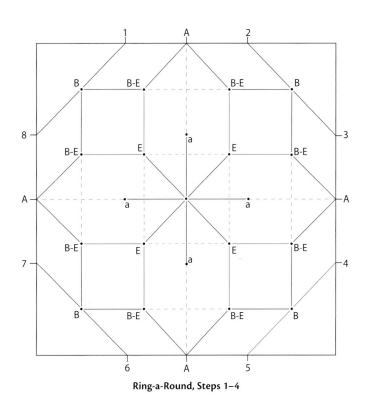

Ring-a-Round, Steps 1–4

Ring-a-Round, continued from page 45

5. To complete the large center diamonds, line up and draw diagonal lines from points **B-E** to **B-E**, breaking in the center area between the **a** points. Repeat around the block (shown in red).

6. Divide the diamonds.

   a. Find the center point of each center and perimeter diamond (page 14) and mark these points with dots.

   b. Line up the center points of diamonds diagonally and draw a dividing line inside each diamond (shown in purple).

   c. Line up the center points of diamonds vertically and draw a dividing line inside each diamond (shown in green).

   d. Line up the center points of diamonds horizontally and draw a dividing line inside each diamond (shown in yellow).

7. Erase any unnecessary guide lines.

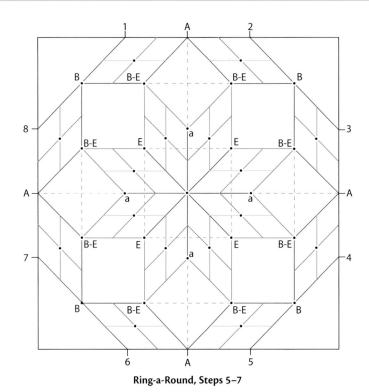

Ring-a-Round, Steps 5–7

FEATHERS

1. Select the grid for your chosen block size using the 8″, 12″, 15″, or 18″ master grids on pullout pages P3–P4 or draw your own grid (page 108). Overlay a sheet of tracing paper and trace the outside **Square A**, markings **1** to **8**, outer **F** marks, and the **A** centers. Referring to **Square F**, mark the **F** points. Lightly draw in the horizontal and vertical centerlines.

2. Start by drawing the spokes of the long feathers (shown in gray) in the center of the block: Line up the path across the center and draw diagonal lines across the center between the **F** points. Draw short vertical and horizontal lines across the center—these will be adjusted later.

3. Next work around the outer edge of the block to draw the long feathers. Refer to the numbers and letters on the master grid to line up a straightedge along the proper path, breaking the lines between the points indicated (shown in gray).

a. Line up and draw vertical and horizontal lines from the outer **F** markings to the **F** points.

b. Line up from an outer **F** marking in the upper left corner across to an outer **F** marking in the lower right corner and draw a diagonal line, breaking in the center area between the vertical and horizontal centerlines. Repeat around the block.

Instructions continue on page 48.

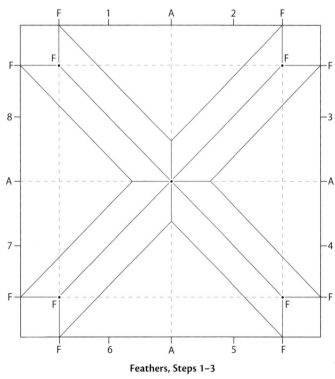

Feathers, Steps 1–3

4. Make the large triangles (shown in blue).

a. Line up and draw diagonal lines across the corners from **A** to **A**, breaking in the center area between the diagonal lines drawn in Step 3b. Mark dots where these lines touch the diagonal lines, to be used later as reference points, and name them **A-F**.

b. Line up and draw vertical and horizontal lines connecting the **A-F** points. Mark dots where these lines cross the vertical and horizontal centers, to be used later as reference points, and name them **y**.

5. Divide the long feathers in half (shown in red).

a. Line up the **A-F** points vertically. Mark new reference points where the straightedge crosses the outer square and name the points **x**. Repeat horizontally.

b. Line up the **x** points vertically and draw short lines inside the long feathers, stopping at the center long diagonal line. Repeat horizontally.

6. Divide the long feathers in half again (shown in green).

a. Line up **x** to **x** diagonally across a corner. Mark dots where the line meets each of the long feather diagonals from Step 3b. Repeat around the block.

b. Line up **y** to **y** diagonally across a corner. Mark dots where the line meets each of the long feather diagonals. Repeat around the block.

c. Line up the new dot marks vertically and horizontally to draw short lines inside the long feathers.

7. Finish extending and connecting lines to complete the block, and erase any unnecessary guide lines.

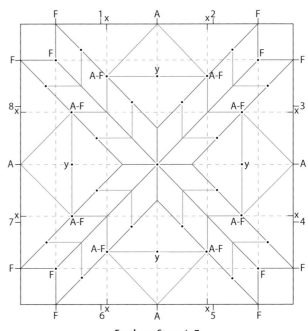

Feathers, Steps 4–7

BASIC ONE-POINT STAND

1. Select the grid for your chosen block size using the 8″, 12″, 15″, or 18″ master grids on pullout pages P3–P4 or draw your own grid (page 108). Overlay a sheet of tracing paper and trace the outside **Square A**, markings **1** to **8**, and the **A** centers. Referring to **Square D** and **Square B**, mark the **D** and **B** points.

2. Start by drawing the spokes of the center diamonds in the center of the block. Refer to the numbers and letters on the master grid to line up a straightedge along the proper path: Line up and draw diagonal lines across the center, between the **D** lines, from **1** to **5**, **2** to **6**, **3** to **7**, and **4** to **8** (shown in gray).

3. Next work around the outer edge of the block.

   a. Line up **A** to the opposite **B** point and draw a line, breaking in the center area between the **D** lines. Repeat around the block (shown in red).

   b. Draw a short diagonal line from the corner to **B**. Repeat around the block (shown in green).

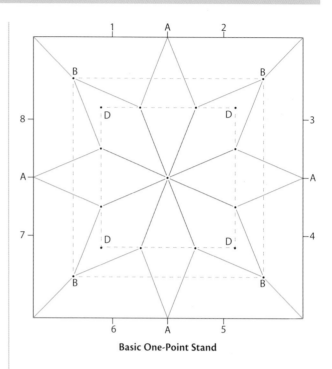

Basic One-Point Stand

DOUBLE STAR

1. Select the grid for your chosen block size using the 8", 12", 15", or 18" master grids on pullout pages P3–P4 or draw your own grid (page 108). Overlay a sheet of tracing paper and trace the outside **Square A**, markings **1** to **8**, and the **A** centers. Referring to **Square E**, **Square D**, and **Square B**, mark the E, D, and **B** points. Lightly draw in the long diagonals.

2. Start by drawing the spokes of the center kites (shown in gray) in the center of the block: Line up the path across the center and darken diagonal lines breaking between **B** and **E** points.

3. Next work around the outer edge of the block. Refer to the numbers and letters on the master grid to line up a straightedge along the proper path, breaking the lines at the points indicated.

a. Line up **A** to the opposite point **B** and draw a line from **A** to point **E**. Repeat around the block to complete 4 on-point kites (shown in red).

b. Line up point **B** to the opposite **A** and draw a line from point **B** to the **D** line (where it meets the on-point kite). Repeat all around the block to complete 4 smaller corner kites (shown in green).

4. Erase any unnecessary guide lines.

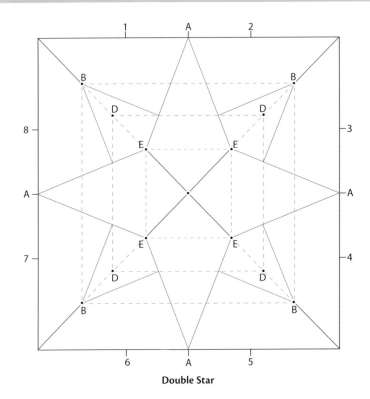

Double Star

MOTH

1. Select the grid for your chosen block size using the 8″, 12″, 15″, or 18″ master grids on pullout pages P3–P4 or draw your own grid (page 108). Overlay a sheet of tracing paper and trace the outside **Square A**, markings **1** to **8**, and the **A** centers.

2. Start by drawing the center configuration (shown in blue) in the center of the block: Line up the path across the center and draw diagonal lines from corner to corner. Draw vertical and horizontal lines across the center from **A** to **A**.

3. Next work around the outer edge of the block. Refer to the numbers and letters on the master grid to line up a straightedge along the proper path, breaking the lines at the points indicated.

   a. Line up **A** to the opposite corner and draw a line from **A** to the long diagonal. Repeat around the block to complete 4 on-point kites (shown in red).

   b. Line up an outer corner to a different opposite **A** and draw a line from the outer corner to meet the on-point kite. Repeat around the block to complete 4 smaller corner kites (shown in green).

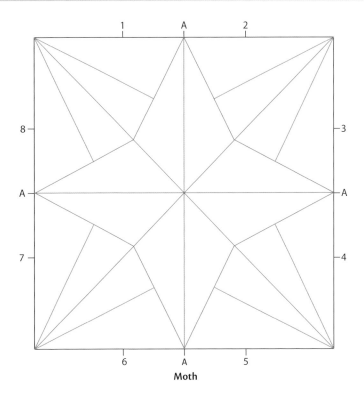

Moth

BLADES

1. Select the grid for your chosen block size using the 8″, 12″, 15″, or 18″ master grids on pullout pages P3–P4 or draw your own grid (page 108). Overlay a sheet of tracing paper and trace the outside **Square A**, markings **1** to **8**, and the **A** centers. Referring to **Square B**, mark the **B** points and lightly draw **Square B**.

2. Start by drawing the spokes of the center kites (shown in gray) in the center of the block: Line up and draw lines across the center, between the **B** lines, from **1** to **5**, **2** to **6**, **3** to **7**, and **4** to **8**.

3. Next work around the outer edge of the block. Refer to the numbers and letters on the master grid to line up a straightedge along the proper path.

   a. Line up and draw short diagonal lines across each corner, through the **B** points, from **2** to **3**, **4** to **5**, **6** to **7**, and **8** to **1** (shown in gray).

   b. Line up and darken diagonal lines across the corners from **A** to **A**, breaking in the center area between the **B** lines (shown in blue).

   c. Line up and darken vertical and horizontal lines from points **B** to **B**, breaking in the center area where the lines drawn in Step 3b meet the **B** line (shown in red).

4. Erase any unnecessary guide lines.

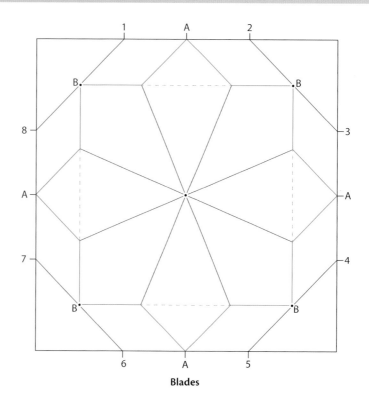

Blades

Variation of Spy block with divided squares in the outer ring

SPY

1. Select the grid for your chosen block size using the 8", 12", 15", or 18" master grids on pullout pages P3–P4 or draw your own grid (page 108). Overlay a sheet of tracing paper and trace the outside **Square A**, markings **1** to **8**, and the **A** centers. Referring to **Square C** and **Square H**, mark the **h** and **H** points. Lightly draw in the horizontal and vertical centerlines and the long diagonal lines.

2. Start by drawing the spokes of the center diamonds (shown in gray) in the center of the block: Draw lines across the center between the **h** points, lining up from **1** to **5**, **2** to **6**, **3** to **7**, and **4** to **8**.

3. Next work around the outer edge of the block. Refer to the numbers and letters on the master grid to line up a straightedge along the proper path, breaking the lines at the points indicated. Line up and draw diagonal lines across each corner from **2** to **3**, **4** to **5**, **6** to **7**, and **8** to **1** (shown in gray).

4. Start the ring of squares (shown in blue).

a. Mark dots on the **H** lines at the horizontal and vertical centers, to be used as reference points, and name them **A-H**.

b. Line up and draw a line from **1** to **3**, breaking between the **A-H** point and the long diagonal. Repeat around the block, connecting **2** to **4**, **5** to **3**, **6** to **4**, **5** to **7**, **6** to **8**, **7** to **1**, and **8** to **2**.

c. Mark dots on the long diagonal lines where the lines drawn in Step 4b meet, to be used as reference points.

Instructions continue on page 56.

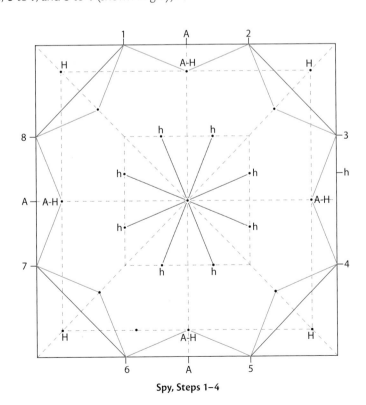

Spy, Steps 1–4

5. Complete the ring of squares and the center diamonds.

a. Line up the center top **A-H** point to the lower right reference point added to the diagonal in Step 4c. Draw a line (shown in red) from point to point, breaking in the center area between the **h** points. Repeat to connect the same **A-H** point with the lower left diagonal reference point.

b. Repeat Step 5a, drawing lines from the center bottom **A-H** point to the top left and right diagonal reference points.

c. Line up the left side **A-H** point to the upper right reference point added to the diagonal in Step 4c. Draw a line (shown in green) from point to point, breaking in the center area between the **h** points. Repeat to connect the same **A-H** point with the lower right diagonal reference point.

d. Repeat Step 5c, drawing lines from the right side **A-H** point to the upper left and lower left diagonal reference points.

6. Erase any unnecessary lines.

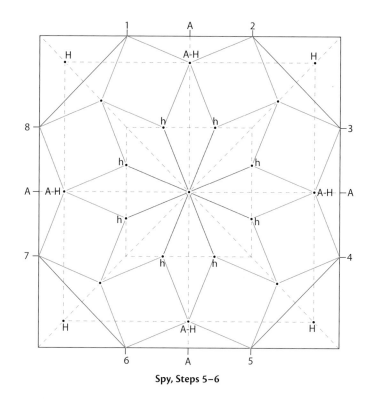

Spy, Steps 5–6

CASTLE WALL

1. Select the grid for your chosen block size using the 8", 12", 15", or 18" master grids on pullout pages P3–P4 or draw your own grid (page 108). Overlay a sheet of tracing paper and trace the outside **Square A**, markings **1** to **8**, outer **G**, **h** and the **A** centers. Referring to **Square C** and **Square G**, mark the inner **h** and **G** points.

2. Start by drawing the spokes of the center half-diamonds (shown in gray) in the center of the block: Draw lines across the center between the **h** points, lining up from **1** to **5**, **2** to **6**, **3** to **7**, and **4** to **8**.

3. Next work around the outer edge of the block. Line up and draw diagonal lines (shown in gray) across each corner from **2** to **3**, **4** to **5**, **6** to **7**, and **8** to **1**.

4. Start the castle wall.

a. Line up the **h** points all around and connect to form an octagonal ring.

b. Line up vertically between the outer **h** marks and draw lines (shown in blue) from the upper **G** line to the lower **G** line, breaking in the center area between the inner **h** points.

c. Line up horizontally between the outer **h** marks and draw lines from the left side **G** line to the right side **G** line, breaking in the center area between the **h** points (shown in blue).

d. Mark dots on the **G** lines, where the lines drawn in Steps 4b and 4c meet them, to be used as reference points, and name them **G-h**.

e. Line up along the **G** lines and draw short lines (shown in gray) across the center, connecting the **G-h** points made in Step 4d.

Instructions continue on page 58.

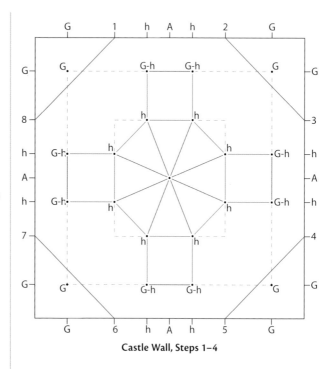

Castle Wall, Steps 1–4

5. Start the outer diamonds (shown in red).

a. Line up **1** to **4**, passing through the **G-h** points, and draw a line, breaking between the **G-h** points. Repeat around the block, using **2** to **7**, **3** to **6**, and **5** to **8**.

b. Line up from **1** to **6** and draw a short line in from each edge, a little longer than the line from **1** to **G-h**. Repeat around the block for **2** to **5**, **3** to **8**, and **4** to **7**.

6. Complete the outer diamonds (shown in green).

a. Line up from an outer **G** marking in the upper left corner across to an outer **G** marking in the lower right corner, passing through 2 **h** points. Draw a line from the point where it touches the vertical line drawn in Step 5b to the first **h** point. Break between the **h** points, and then draw a line from the second **h** point to the point where it touches the horizontal line drawn in Step 5b. Mark dots to be used as reference points where these lines meet. Repeat around the block.

b. Line up the reference points made in Step 6a diagonally across the corners and draw lines to connect them to complete the corner squares.

7. Erase any unnecessary guide lines.

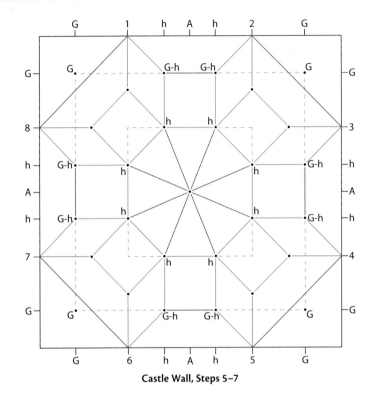

Castle Wall, Steps 5–7

BUTTE

1. Select the grid for your chosen block size using the 8″, 12″, 15″, or 18″ master grids on pullout pages P3–P4 or draw your own grid (page 108). Overlay a sheet of tracing paper and trace the outside **Square A**, markings **1** to **8**, and the **A** centers. Referring to **Square D** and **Square B**, mark the **D** and **B** points.

2. Start by drawing the center spokes (shown in gray): Line up and draw lines across the center, between the **D** lines from **1** to **5**, **2** to **6**, **3** to **7**, and **4** to **8**. Mark a dot where these lines meet the **D** lines, to be used as reference points.

3. Next work around the outer edge of the block. Refer to the numbers and letters on the master grid to line up a straightedge along the proper path: Line up and draw diagonal lines (shown in gray) across each corner from **2** to **3**, **4** to **5**, **6** to **7**, and **8** to **1**, passing through points **B**.

4. Complete the 4 large diamonds (shown in blue): Line up from **A** to the opposite **B** point and draw a line from **A** to the first reference point (from Step 2) it meets. Repeat around the block.

5. Complete 4 half-diamonds (shown in red): Line up the reference points made in Step 2 diagonally across the corners and draw lines to connect them.

6. Erase any unnecessary guide lines.

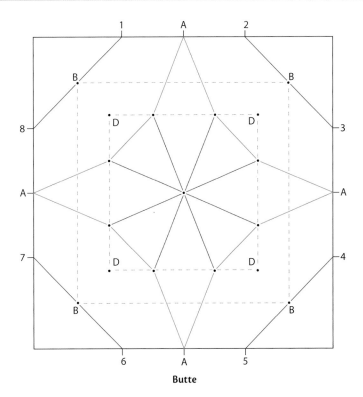

Butte

EVEN

1. Select the grid for your chosen block size using the 8″, 12″, 15″, or 18″ master grids on pullout pages P3–P4 or draw your own grid (page 108). Overlay a sheet of tracing paper and trace the outside **Square A**, markings **1** to **8**, and the **A** centers. Referring to **Square D** and **Square B**, mark the inner **D** and **B** points.

2. Start by drawing the spokes of the block (shown in gray) in the center of the block: Line up and draw lines across the center from **1** to **5**, **2** to **6**, **3** to **7**, and **4** to **8**. Mark points on these lines where they cross the **D** lines, to be used as reference points.

3. Next work around the outer edge of the block. Refer to the numbers and letters on the master grid to line up a straightedge along the proper path: Line up and draw diagonal lines (shown in gray) across each corner from **2** to **3**, **4** to **5**, **6** to **7**, and **8** to **1**, passing through points **B**.

4. Connect the reference points that were added to the **D** lines in Step 2 all around to form the center octagon (blue).

5. Line up and draw a line (shown in red) from **A** to the opposite **B** point, breaking in the center area between the reference points from Step 2. Repeat around the block.

6. Erase any unnecessary guide lines.

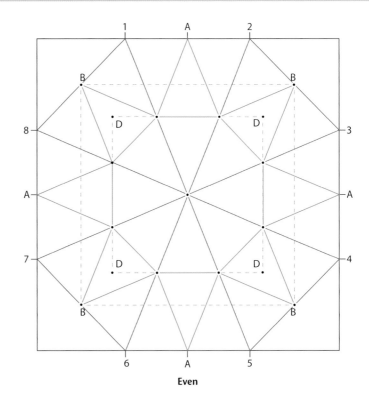

Even

FORBIDDEN FRUIT

1. Select the grid for your chosen block size using the 8″, 12″, 15″, or 18″ master grids on pullout pages P3–P4 or draw your own grid (page 108). Overlay a sheet of tracing paper and trace the outside **Square A**, outer markings **1** to **8**, and the **A** centers. Referring to **Square D** and **Square B**, mark the **D** and **B** inner points.

2. Start by drawing the spokes (shown in gray) in the center of the block: Line up and draw lines across the block from **3** to **7** and **4** to **8**. Line up and draw lines across the center from **1** toward **5** and from **2** toward **6**, but stopping at the **D** line before reaching **5** and **6**. Mark points on these lines where they meet or cross the **D** lines, to be used later as reference points.

3. Next work around the outer edge of the block. Refer to the numbers and letters on the master grid to line up a straightedge along the proper path: Line up and draw diagonal lines (shown in gray) across the upper corners from **2** to **3** and **8** to **1**, passing through points **B.**

4. Complete 8 large diamonds (shown in blue). Note the 2 diamonds in the lower left and right corner areas are lightly drawn for reference. They will be erased later.

Line up from the lower A to the opposite B point and draw a line, breaking in the center area between the D lines. Repeat around the block. This is the same construction used for a Basic One-Point Stand block, Step 3 (page 49).

Instructions continue on page 62.

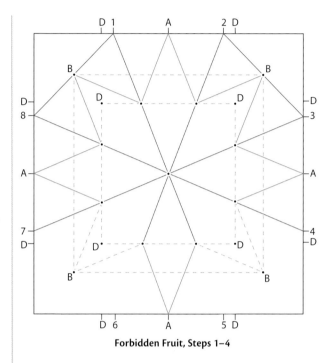

Forbidden Fruit, Steps 1–4

✳ NOTE

A protractor is a useful tool when drawing this block. Use it in Step 7a to be certain the sides of the trunk are perpendicular to the bottom of the outside square. It is also helpful when drawing the lines in Step 7c at a 45° angle.

Forbidden Fruit, continued from page 61

5. Divide the large diamonds.

a. Find the center point of each the 8 large diamonds (page 14). Mark the center points with a dot (shown in red).

b. Line up the center points of the large diamonds diagonally and draw dividing lines inside each diamond (shown in red). Do not draw dividing lines in the lower left and lower right large diamonds.

c. Extend the lines you have just made to the top and side edges and to the diagonal corner lines on each of the 5 large upper diamonds to create 10 small half-diamonds, 2 in each of the top 5 wedges. (shown in green).

6. Finish drawing the remaining outer small diamonds and half-diamonds started in Step 5c.

a. The long diagonal line from **1** to the center must be divided equally into 4 parts. Two of these divisions are on the line already. Divide the larger space between 1 and the elbows of the 2 large diamonds in half. Refer to Dividing a Line in Half (page 14) and mark a dot (shown in green) to be used as a reference point. Repeat to divide the lines from outer points 7, 8, 2, 3 and 4 to the center to mark a total of 6 green dots..

b. Line up and draw lines (shown in yellow) from the reference points made in Step 6a to the ends of the extended lines made in Step 5c. Repeat all around to make a total of 4 of these divisions.

c. Line up and draw lines (shown in purple) from the reference points made in Step 6a to where the green lines from Step 5c meet the outer edge of the block. Repeat to make a total of 6 purple lines, as shown.

7. Draw the tree trunk.

a. Line up vertically with the side elbow of the small diamond just left of center (marked **Y** on the diagram) and draw a trunk line from the **Y** reference point to the lower edge (see Note, page 61). Repeat on the right side.

b. Extend the **1-to-5** and **2-to-6** lines made in Step 2 down to the trunk lines drawn in Step 7a.

c. Line up a 45° line from the outside 6 mark with the trunk line, and draw a line to create a small triangle.at the base of the trunk (see Note, page 61). Repeat on the other side of the trunk, connecting outside mark 5 to the trunk at a 45° angle.

8. Erase the 2 large diamonds in the bottom left and right corners and any other guidelines you drew.

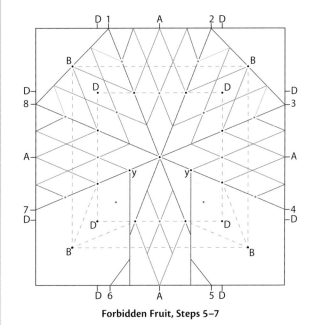

Forbidden Fruit, Steps 5–7

Silk Wood Blocks, 52" × 44", 2011

The overall design is original, based on blocks dating back to the 1800s. The luster of the silken Oakshott fabric makes each block glow. I used quarter-yard pieces of this fabric. The quilt is machine-pieced with set-in seams, machine-outline-quilted, and hand-quilted.

Blocks Used:					
Basic One-Point Stand (page 49)	**Snow Crystals** (page 30)	**Magical** (page 36)	**Blades** (page 54)	**Enigma** (page 52)	**Basic Two-Point Stand** (page 17)
Ring-a-Round (page 45)	**Onstar** (page 18)	**Two-Point-One** (page 21)	**Ball** (page 22)	**Three Rings** (page 35)	**1922** (page 26)
Fan (page 23)	**Corner Half** (page 43)	**Even** (page 60)	**Rolling** (page 42)	**Starbrite** (page 28)	**Dutch Rose** (page 38)
Whirl (page 53)	**Swallows** (page 19)	**Kite Tails** (page 34)	**Castle Wall** (page 57)	**Fish** (page 40)	**Carp** (page 32)
Peony (page 25)	**Spy** (page 55)	**Bat** (page 24)	**Star Shower** (page 29)	**Facets** (page 20)	**Forbidden Fruit** (page 61)

 The blocks for the star quilts in this book are made up of various shapes to which unique letters or numbers have been assigned. Many of the shapes, such as triangle B, are common among the blocks in the book. That means triangle B is the same on all the blocks it is used on, as long as the blocks used are all the same size (such as 8" square). The pieces for the blocks are cut from freezer-paper templates made of these shapes, although some shapes, such as squares and triangles, are easily cut without templates. Refer to the block piecing chart (pages 75–86) and the block cutting chart (pages 87 and 88) to find out which shapes you will use in your chosen blocks, which are common among the blocks, and which templates you will need. Use the information to plan your project and streamline your cutting and piecing. *Commonalities* (page 96) is a great example of making use of these common shapes among blocks. As you begin to design your own blocks, you should also assign numbers and letters to their unique shapes.

The template making and fabric cutting methods provided are fast, easy, and efficient. There is minimal waste of fabric and no need to trim down units after sewing them. The freezer-paper templates can be reused a number of times. You don't need any unique tools or plastic templates to cut your fabrics into the needed shapes.

Fabric Considerations

Following are a few simple guidelines for selecting fabric for star quilts:

- Use high-quality, interesting fabric.

- Make sure the fabric is not so busy that it eclipses the graceful detail of the block's design.

- Make sure the design of the block and the fabric work together for an easy-to-look-at quilt.

The quilts in this book are based on a planned, scrappy use of fabric. Some of the quilts were made from purchased collections of fabric and some from my own stash of quarter- and eighth-yard cuts. You can use cotton or silk (see Working with Silk, page 65).

When selecting fabric, I start with black-and-white thumbnail sketches of my blocks—no shading or color. I begin by making a few fabric choices from the stack I want to work with. I start by planning the center of the quilt. I then audition the "supporting cast." If it is a multi-block quilt, I sew parts of several blocks together and refine the arrangement process. I have two things to consider: the line drawing of the block(s) and the atmosphere created by the fabric.

At this point, I start to work in what I consider to be background fabric for the center stars. This is fabric that will help to tie the blocks together. It may be one, two, or many pieces of fabric that have something in common.

I continue selecting from my stack of chosen fabric and complete the blocks. I line them up following my original thumbnail sketch and make any adjustments that may be necessary now that color has become part of the equation.

I explore sashing and framing after the blocks are complete. I don't even begin to look at fabric for this use until my interior blocks are complete. This keeps in play the planned, scrappy look that I find appealing. To see the effects of framing the blocks, I compare the placement of the exact same blocks first on a light background and then on a dark background and then decide which effect I prefer.

Silk is wonderful, but it can be a little challenging to work with. I have two different techniques for working with silk. There are pros and cons to each method.

Before cutting or sewing silk, I spritz it with water and press it. This helps to preshrink it and allows me to check for colorfastness. It also gives me a chance to enjoy looking at and touching it.

Technique 1—Lightweight Stabilizer

One technique for handling silk involves preparing it with a lightweight iron-on (fusible) stabilizer (see Resources, page 111) before use. Any block can be constructed using this technique.

1. Back all of the silk with lightweight iron-on stabilizer using a pressing cloth, before cutting out the pieces.

2. Sew the pieces together.

3. Use a non-stick pressing sheet like parchment paper or a silicone sheet when pressing the seams so as to avoid an imprint or damage to the fabric. Peek under the pressing cloth as needed to make sure the seams are flat and, if they are pressed to the side, that they are oriented in the proper direction.

Technique 2—Paper-Guided Piecing

The silk used in blocks constructed using paper-guided piecing (page 72) is temporarily ironed to a piece of freezer paper. This allows the fabric preparation, sewing, and pressing to progress very quickly. The only drawback is that the paper-guided piecing method can be used only for blocks without set-in seams; sometimes blocks can be modified to suit the technique by adding seams to eliminate set-in seams or by changing the order of assembly.

Making Templates

Make templates for all of the shapes on the master pattern(s) you plan to use. If you prefer, squares, rectangles, half-square triangles, and quarter-square triangles can be cut without templates. Refer to Cutting Techniques (page 68).

1. Place your accurately drawn master pattern on a smooth work surface.

2. Place a piece of freezer paper, paper side up, on top of the master pattern.

3. Use a straightedge to trace the exact outline of the template shape.

4. Use a short rotary cutting ruler with a ¼" grid to draw an exact ¼" seam allowance around the template.

5. Cut out the template.

6. Repeat Steps 1–5 to make additional copies as needed.

7. Assign a number or letter to the templates and note the block size. It may also be helpful to put a grainline reference on the templates.

Cutting Fabric Pieces

I use either a short rotary cutting ruler with freezer-paper templates or a standard rotary cutting ruler without templates to cut my fabric. The method I choose depends on how many pieces I need and their shape. When I want to cut a few pieces at a time to achieve a scrappy look in the center star unit or for the irregular shapes near the outer edges of a block, I use templates. When I need a few of each shape, but not a long fabric strip, I use two or more templates and cut pieces from a stack of up to four short strips. And when I need many pieces of common shapes, such as diamonds, squares, and triangles, I speed cut from a strip of fabric, relying on the standard rotary cutting ruler.

Speed Cutting

Use this method to cut large numbers of similar-size pieces in common shapes—such as diamonds, squares, and triangles—from long strips of fabric. In fact, with a little preplanning you can cut large numbers of most of the template pieces from premeasured strips. I prefer to cut my strips on the lengthwise grain. Also, I usually leave the points on my pieces and trim them after sewing. If you choose to go with a pretrimmed piece, adjust the strip width.

1. Cut strips of fabric the required width and fabric grain as specified in the project.

2. Then cut them into the required number of pieces. You may choose to use a template or cut out the shapes without one.

Speed Cutting Diamonds along a 22½° Edge

To speed cut diamonds on the lengthwise grain, cut them along an edge cut on an angle 22½° from the lengthwise grain. Refer to Creating a 22½° Angle Edge (page 67).

1. Cut a piece of fabric along a lengthwise edge on a 22½° angle.

2. Place a freezer-paper diamond along the 22½° edge to determine the width of the strip you need to cut. Line up a standard rotary cutting ruler along the cut 22½° angle edge and cut a strip slightly larger (⅛") than the width of the diamond.

3. Cut additional strips and stack if you will be cutting many diamonds.

4. Diamonds will be cut off the strip at a 45° angle. To set up the strip for this orientation, make a first clean-up cut at an end of the strip at a 45° angle. From this point you will cut the proper size diamonds from the strip. Use either the freezer-paper template as a guide or a standard rotary ruler that has a 45° angle marked on it. Align the 45° angle line on the strip at the proper width and cut.

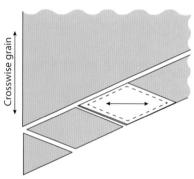

Speed cutting diamonds along a 22½° angle edge

Cutting Squares and Rectangles

You can cut squares and rectangles using freezer-paper templates as described above, or if you prefer you can follow the steps below and cut the fabric without templates.

1. Measure the square or rectangle on the master pattern.

2. Add a ¼" seam allowance all around the piece.

3. The new square or rectangle will be ½" longer in each direction than it is on the master pattern. Note this size on the master pattern for easy reference.

4. Use a short rotary cutting ruler to cut the pieces on the straight grain of the fabric.

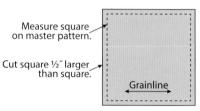

Cutting a square

Cutting Triangles

It is important to pay attention to the grain of the fabric when working with triangles so that the outside edges of finished blocks and setting triangles will be on the straight grain. Refer to Grainline Placement (page 66).

Half-Square Triangles

Half-square triangles, such as triangle B, used in a number of the blocks in this book, are used mostly for the outer corners of blocks or for settings. For these triangles you can draw freezer-paper templates (page 65), or if you prefer you can follow the steps below and cut the fabric without templates.

1. Measure across the short edge of the corner or setting triangle on the master pattern.

2. Add ⅞" to this measurement to find the size of the square you will need to cut.

3. Use a short rotary cutting ruler to cut 2 squares per block on the straight grain of the fabric.

4. Cut a square diagonally in half.

5. Cut the second square in half, this time cutting diagonally in the opposite direction. This will produce 4 corner squares with the proper orientation of the grainline.

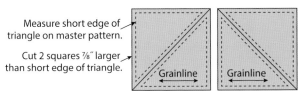

Measure short edge of triangle on master pattern.

Cut 2 squares ⅞″ larger than short edge of triangle.

Grainline Grainline

Cut squares diagonally in opposite directions to make 4 corner triangles.

Cutting half-square triangles

Quarter-Square Triangles

Quarter-square triangles, such as triangle F, used in a number of the blocks in this book, are used along the sides of blocks or settings. For these triangles you can draw freezer-paper templates (page 65), or if you prefer you can follow the steps below and cut the fabric without templates.

1. Measure along the long edge of the triangle on the master pattern.

2. Add 1¼″ to this measurement to find the size of the square you will need.

3. Use a short rotary cutting ruler to cut a square for every 4 triangles you require, on the straight grain of the fabric.

4. Cut this square diagonally in each direction. This will produce 4 triangles per square.

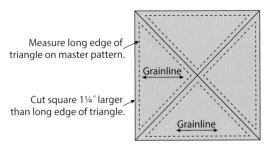

Measure long edge of triangle on master pattern.

Grainline

Cut square 1¼″ larger than long edge of triangle.

Grainline

Cutting quarter-square triangles

TRIMMING POINTS

I have often puzzled over how to trim points for ease in piecing. It's not necessary to trim points. Some people think it helps the piecing process and some do not. If you prefer to trim, I have devised a simple way to do this using just a short rotary cutting ruler.

Diamonds and Kites

For 45° points found on diamonds, triangles, kites, and some irregular shapes, I line up the crosshairs on my ruler at the sewing point. I measure ⅜″ beyond the perpendicular sewing point and trim off the corner straight across.

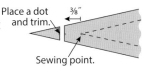

Trim. ⅜″ 45°

Sewing point.

Trimming diamond points

Irregular Shapes

The tight angles on some irregular shapes are a bit trickier. The same measurements of ⅜″ and ¼″ are used, but they are angled a little differently. Measure ⅜″ beyond the perpendicular sewing point as above. Place a center point dot for future reference, and then trim off the excess.

Place a dot and trim. ⅜″

Sewing point.

Trimming irregular points

The piece can be used as is or you can further trim an angle at the reference point dot.

1. Measure along the outside cut edges of the piece and place dots on the outside edges ¼″ from and perpendicular to the sewing line.

2. Line up the ruler to connect the center dot to each side dot and trim off the corners.

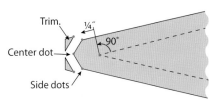

Trim. ¼″ 90°

Center dot

Side dots

Further trimming irregular points (optional)

Piecing Techniques

The blocks in this book can be pieced together easily and accurately by following a few general guidelines. See Piecing a Center Star (below) and Piecing a Square or Triangle to a Center Star (page 71). Then refer to Block Piecing Guide (pages 74–86) for specific instructions on piecing together the blocks you are making. Some blocks also may be pieced together using Paper-Guided Piecing (page 72).

PIECING A CENTER STAR

Start with the center of the block, which usually contains diamonds, half-diamonds, or kites. A star is usually made up of 4 or 8 pieces that meet in the center. This is the focal point of the block and accuracy is important here. The instructions below are for an 8-diamond center star.

1. Mark the stitching corners at the elbows with a dot. These are the stopping points. Mark the stopping points on all the diamonds for the center star.

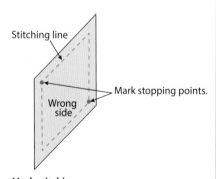

Mark stitching corners.

2. Put 2 diamonds right sides together and stitch from point to elbow. Stop stitching at the marked dot and backstitch 3 stitches. Do not cut the thread. Raise the needle and presser foot.

3. Put 2 more diamonds right sides together. Fit them under the raised presser foot close to the first pair of diamonds. Stitch from point to elbow, stopping and backstitching as before. Repeat for the remaining 2 pairs of diamonds to make 4 pairs.

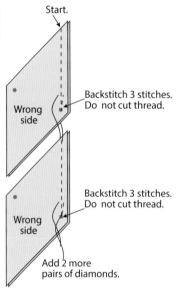

Join diamonds.

4. Press the seams open and cut the paired diamonds apart. Trim away the threads.

5. Put 2 pairs of diamonds right sides together and join them by stitching down a side from point to the elbow. Backstitch 3 stitches. Do not cut the thread. Feed in 2 more pairs of diamonds as in Step 3 and stitch them together the same way. Cut the thread.

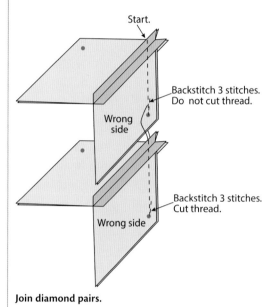

Join diamond pairs.

6. Press the seams open and cut the diamonds apart. Trim away the corners and the threads. You now have 2 halves of the center star pieced.

7. Put the 2 halves right sides together, lining up the centers exactly—fold back the seam allowance and peek to be sure. Pin about ¼" away from each side of the center seam, and pin at each elbow and in the spaces between (about 6 pins).

8. Start sewing at an elbow by inserting the machine needle exactly through the marked dot. Sew forward 3 stitches, backstitch 3 stitches, and continue to the other elbow. Stop at the far elbow dot, and backstitch 3 stitches.

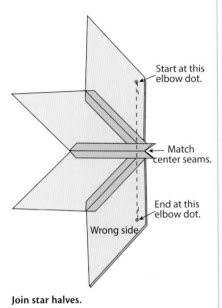

Start at this elbow dot.

Match center seams.

End at this elbow dot.

Wrong side

Join star halves.

9. Remove the completed star and examine the center seam joins. Correct any misalignment. Trim corners and threads, and press the seam open.

PIECING A SQUARE OR TRIANGLE TO A CENTER STAR

Set-in seams, such as those used to piece squares to a center diamond unit, are used for many of the blocks in this book. Fortunately, they are not difficult to master, and I chain piece these as I do other units. Follow these steps for attaching a triangle or an irregular shape to a center star unit. You can use this method to attach a corner shape to any piece with inside corners.

1. With right sides together, place a square under a diamond in the center star unit. Pin the diamond to the square at the diamond point. Align the raw edges of the diamond and the square down to the diamond elbow stopping point. Pin the layers together, right through the elbow stopping point. Add more pins if necessary to hold the pieces in place.

2. Sew from the diamond point to the elbow. Stop at the marked dot and backstitch 3 stitches. Raise the needle and presser foot. Cut the thread (or continue to chain piece the next block).

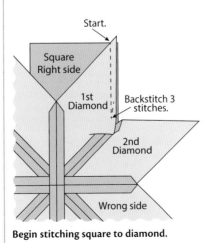

Start.

Square Right side

1st Diamond

Backstitch 3 stitches.

2nd Diamond

Wrong side

Begin stitching square to diamond.

3. Rotate the pieces at the elbow, ready to place the next diamond in the center star. Put a pin through the elbow of the next diamond and through the corner of the square just sewn. Align the raw edges of the next diamond and the side of the square to the diamond point. Continue to pin along this next sewing line, pinning the end of the diamond point to the square underneath.

4. Sew from the elbow dot, backstitching, and continue to the end point of the diamond. Press toward the triangles or squares.

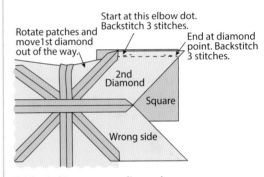

Rotate patches and move 1st diamond out of the way.

Start at this elbow dot. Backstitch 3 stitches.

End at diamond point. Backstitch 3 stitches.

2nd Diamond

Square

Wrong side

Finish stitching square to diamond.

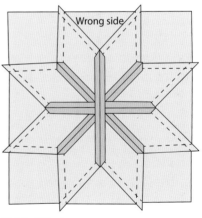

Wrong side

Finished block

PAPER-GUIDED PIECING

Paper-guided piecing is a great way to piece accurately, especially when using silk fabric. As a bonus, because you are folding back the freezer paper when you sew, there is no paper to tear out of the seams, and you can reuse the freezer paper! The technique works especially well for blocks that do not have set-in seams, such as Moth (page 51), Whirl (page 53), and Even (page 60). Many blocks, such as Snow Crystals (page 30), Carp (page 32), Basic Two-Point Stand (page 17), and Basic One-Point Stand (page 49), can be modified to suit this technique by adding seams to eliminate set-in seams and changing the order of assembly. In addition, some blocks, such as Two-Point-One (page 21), can be pieced using a combination of traditional and paper-guided piecing methods.

Paper-guided piecing template patterns for all the above blocks in the 8″ × 8″ size are given in *Eight Eights* Templates for Paper-Guided Piecing (pattern pullout page P2). If you are working in a larger block size, create your own template pattern using the given ones as a guide.

Start with the Master Pattern

1. Make sure each piece of your chosen block pattern is identified with a number or letter in a logical piecing order. The paper-guided piecing technique does not produce the reversed design found in many traditional paper-piecing methods.

2. Draw a master template onto plain paper by tracing each unit and the shapes within it. Make sure to leave at least 1″ between the units on the piece of paper. Number the pieces as on the template. Cut out each of the units, leaving about a ½″ border around each.

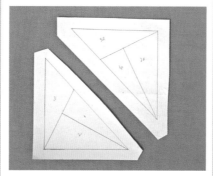
Trace and label units.

3. Make the freezer-paper templates by stacking 4 pieces of freezer paper, shiny side up, under each of the plain paper units. Turn the stack over to heat baste all 5 pieces together.

4. Put the stack right side up on the sewing machine and sew along all lines with an unthreaded needle.

Sew along all lines.

5. Gently separate the traced plain paper guide from the stack. This can be left intact for future use or cut apart and used for guides to rough cut fabric patches (see Prep Work, below). Transfer the piece numbers from the plain paper to the freezer-paper templates. *The freezer paper will be a mirror image of the plain paper, so number accordingly.*

6. Keep the freezer paper sections/ quadrants intact, but trim off any extra along the edges—these pieces have no seam allowance.

Prep Work

1. Cut out the fabric pieces. The easiest way is to cut apart the plain paper pieces from Step 5 (above) and place them right side up on the right side of a stack of fabric; roughly cut out the fabric pieces, adding about ½″ seam allowance all around.

2. Clip or pin the plain paper guide on top of the rough-cut stacks of fabric to help keep them organized.

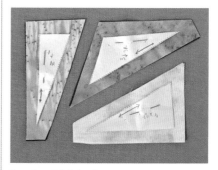
Rough-cut fabric pieces

3. Crease along the perforations of the freezer-paper sections by folding back and forth.

Sewing the Basic Units

1. Center the outline of a shape 1 over the fabric and securely press the shiny side of the freezer paper to the wrong side of fabric piece 1.

Press shape 1 onto fabric piece 1.

2. Fold back the matte/dull side of the freezer paper along the perforation between pieces 1 and 2. Release any of fabric 1 that goes over the fold-back.

3. Slip fabric piece 2 under fabric piece 1, right sides together. Make sure the piece is covered by freezer paper. Hold the fabrics up to the light to check.

4. Make sure the freezer paper is stuck tight at the fold, and sew along the edge of the freezer paper to join pieces 1 and 2.

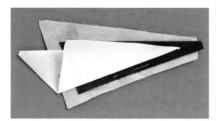

Fold back freezer paper and place fabric 2 under fabric 1.

Sew close to freezer-paper fold.

5. Trim the fabric seam allowance to ¼".

6. Press the seam in the desired direction. This is easily accomplished by lifting the freezer paper slightly. Be sure to press the seam without any puckers, folds, or creases.

7. Press the freezer paper flat over pieces 1 and 2. If your seam is a little off, you can lift the freezer paper and gently adjust.

8. Proceed to fabric piece 3 and continue as above.

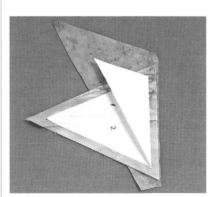

Add fabric 3. Reverse unit shown.

9. Complete the units. Do not remove the freezer paper.

Joining the Basic Units to Make Larger Units

1. Arrange the completed units to view what the completed piece will look like.

2. Align 2 units right sides together.

3. Pin through the seam allowance close to, but not through, the freezer paper.

4. Fold the edge of the bottom piece of freezer paper back about ¼" along the seamline.

5. Flip over and sew along the edge of the top piece of freezer paper.

Fold bottom freezer paper back along seamline.

Sew along edge of top piece of freezer paper.

6. Press the seam allowance in the preferred direction.

> **✳ NOTE**
>
> For the paper-guided quilt projects in this book (pages 100-105), the template pieces are provided on pattern pullout P2). Refer to the project instructions for template information.

7. Lift and press the freezer paper flat to the fabric.

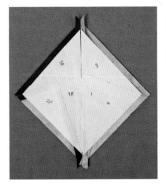

Wrong side

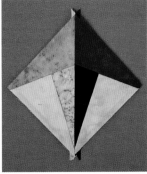

Right side

8. Continue as above until all the pieces are joined to the block.

9. Trim the outer edges of the completed block to a ¼" seam allowance.

10. Gently remove the intact freezer-paper pattern and store for additional blocks.

Finished block (wrong side)

Finished block (right side)

BLOCK PIECING GUIDE

Refer to Cutting (page 65), Piecing Techniques (page 70), Piecing a Center Star (page 70), Piecing a Square or Triangle to a Center Star (page 71), and Paper-Guided Piecing (page 72) for general piecing instructions.

Using a Block Design from this Book

1. Choose the design and size for the blocks to be used in your project and draw a master pattern for each block design (see How to Draw the Blocks, page 12).

2. Locate the blocks in the Block Piecing Chart (page 75) to see what unique shapes are used. Each unique shape is assigned a number or a letter. If you are making 2 different blocks, refer to the Block Cutting Chart (page 87) to see if they share a shape. You may want to cut out these pieces at the same time (but only if the blocks are the same size). Make note of which shapes will require a template for cutting and which shapes can be cut from measurements.

3. Refer to the images in the chart and cut out the pieces you need.

4. Consult the Block Piecing Chart (page 75) for specific block assembly instructions to construct the blocks. Notice the blocks have red and green dots, which you may find helpful. A red dot at the end of a seam or intersection indicates to stop and backstitch; do not sew into the seam allowance. A green dot at the end of a seam or an intersection indicates to continue stitching past the green dot to the end of the fabric. If making several blocks, consider piecing to save time.

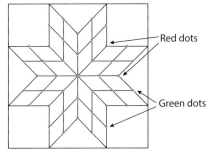

Red dots

Green dots

Red: Stop and backstitch.
Green: Continue to sew through to end of fabric.

5. Press as you go. I prefer to press the seams on the center stars open.

6. Assemble the blocks and finish the project as you like.

Using Your Own Block Design

Follow the same method as above, but because the block is your own design, you will need to determine which shapes you need. When constructing the block, in general, you will work from the center outward, beginning with the center star unit. Piece any subunits as far as you can and then join them to the center star. Look for similar blocks on the Block Piecing Chart to help you plan your work.

BLOCK PIECING CHART

First use this chart to find the shapes you'll need for your chosen blocks and the instructions to assemble the blocks. Then refer to the Block Cutting Chart (page 87) as needed to help plan your cutting.

SHAPES USED	BLOCK INSTRUCTIONS	ASSEMBLY DIAGRAM
	Basic Two-Point Stand	
	1. Sew 8 diamonds "15" together to make the center star. **2.** Sew a triangle "F" to top, bottom, and sides of center star. **3.** Sew a square "A" to each corner of center star.	
	Onstar	
	1. Sew 4 diamonds "8" together to make a diamond unit. Repeat to make 8 diamond units. **2.** Sew 8 diamond units together to make the center star. **3.** Sew a triangle "F" to top, bottom, and sides of center star. **4.** Sew a square "A" to each corner of center star.	
	Swallows	
	1. Sew 3 diamonds "5" and 4 triangles "sm" together to make a diamond unit. Repeat to make 8 diamond units. **2.** Sew 8 diamond units together to make the center star. **3.** Sew a triangle "F" to top, bottom, and sides of center star. **4.** Sew a square "A" to each corner of center star.	

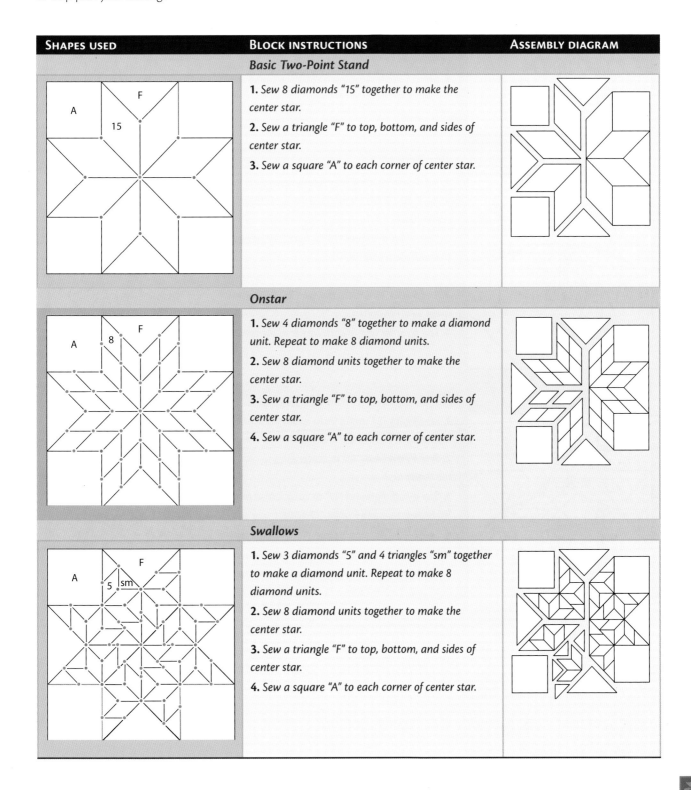

1922

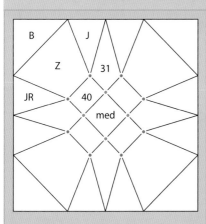

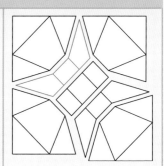

1. Sew a rectangle "40" to 2 opposite sides of square "med" to make a "40-med-40" unit.

2. Sew a kite "31" to each short side of a rectangle "40." Repeat to make 2 units "31-40-31" (shown in blue).

3. Sew a "31-40-31" unit to each side of the "40-med-40" unit to make the center star.

4. Sew a piece "J" to a side of piece "Z" and a piece "JR" to the other side. Add a triangle "B." Repeat to make 4 corner units.

5. Sew a corner unit to each corner of the center star.

Starlight

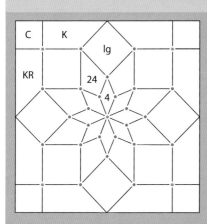

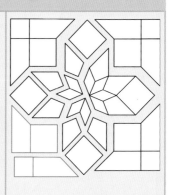

1. Sew 8 diamonds "4" together to make the center diamond unit.

2. Sew a kite "24" between each pair of center diamonds "4" to complete the center star.

3. Sew a square "lg" to top, bottom, and sides of the center star.

4. Sew a piece "K" to a square "lg" (shown in blue). Sew a piece "KR" to square "C" (shown in red). Sew these 2 units together. Repeat to make 4 corner units.

5. Sew a corner unit to each corner of the center star.

Starbrite

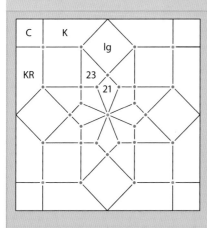

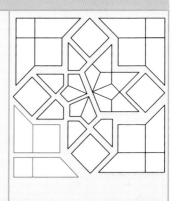

1. Sew 8 kites "21" together to make the center diamond unit.

2. Sew a kite "23" between each pair of center kites "21" to complete the center star.

3. Sew a square "lg" to top, bottom, and sides of the center star.

4. Sew a piece "K" to a square "lg" (shown in blue). Sew a piece "KR" to square "C" (shown in red). Sew these 2 units together. Repeat to make 4 corner units.

5. Sew a corner unit to each corner of the center star.

Star Shower

1. Sew 8 diamonds "11" together to make the center star.

2. Sew a square "lg" to top, bottom, and sides of the center star.

3. Sew a piece "L" to a side of kite "32" and a piece "LR" to the other side. Repeat to make 4 corner units.

4. Sew a corner unit to each corner of the center star.

Snow Crystals

1. Sew 8 diamonds "8" together to make the center star.

2. Sew a square "sm" to top, bottom, and sides of the center star. Set aside.

3. Sew 4 diamonds "8" together to make a 4-diamond unit (shown in blue). Add a square "C" and 2 triangles "E" to the unit (shown in red).

4. Sew a diamond "8" to each side of a square "sm" to make an "8-sm-8" unit (shown in green). Sew the "8-sm-8" unit to the 4-diamond unit.

5. Repeat Steps 3 and 4 to make 4 corner units.

6. Sew a corner unit to each side of the center star.

7. Add a rectangle "D" to the top, bottom, and sides to complete the block.

Carp

1. Sew 8 diamonds "8" together to make the center star.

2. Sew a square "sm" to top, bottom, and sides of the center star. Set aside.

3. Sew 6 diamonds "8" together to make a 6-diamond unit (shown in blue). Add 4 squares "C" and 2 triangles "E" to the unit to make a corner unit (shown in red). Repeat to make 4 corner units.

4. Sew a corner unit to each side of the center star.

5. Sew the seam between the corner units to join them together at the sides.

Kite Tails

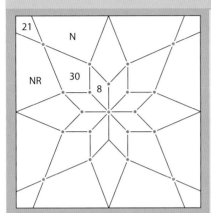

1. Sew 8 diamonds "8" together to make the center diamond unit.

2. Sew a kite "30" to top, bottom, and sides of the center diamond unit.

3. Sew a piece "N" to a kite "21" (shown in blue). Sew a piece "NR" to a kite "30" (shown in red). Sew these 2 units together to make a corner unit. Repeat to make 4 corner units.

4. Sew a corner unit to each corner of the center diamond unit.

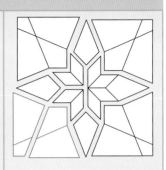

Three Rings

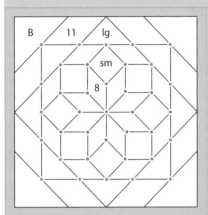

1. Sew 8 diamonds "8" together to make the center diamond unit.

2. Sew a square "sm" between each pair of center diamonds "8."

3. Sew a diamond "8" between each pair of squares "sm" all around the center unit.

4. Sew a triangle "lg" to top, bottom, and sides of the center diamond unit.

5. Sew a diamond "11" to each side of a triangle "lg" (shown in blue). Add a triangle "B" to make a corner unit. Repeat to make 4 corner units.

6. Sew a corner unit to each corner of the center unit.

Magical

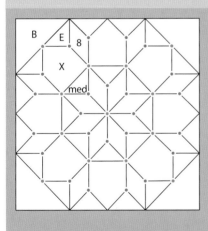

1. Sew 8 diamonds "8" together to make the center star.

2. Sew a triangle "med" to a house piece "X" to make a house unit (shown in blue). Repeat to make 4 house units.

3. Sew a triangle "med" to another house piece "X," as in Step 2. Sew a diamond "8" to each side of the house piece (shown in red). Repeat to make 4 house-corner units.

4. Sew a house unit (blue) to the top, bottom, and sides of the center star.

5. Sew a house-corner unit (red) to each corner of the center star.

6. Sew 16 triangles "E" around the block.

7. Sew a triangle "B" to each of the corners of the block.

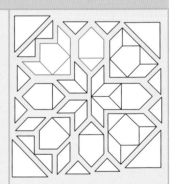

Dutch Rose

1. Sew 8 diamonds "8" together to make the center star.

2. Sew 2 diamonds "8" together. Add a square "sm" (shown in blue). Repeat to make 4 "8-sm-8" units.

3. Sew an "8-sm-8" unit to the top, bottom, and sides of the center star.

4. Sew a piece "V" and a piece "VR" together to make a V-shaped unit (shown in red).

5. Sew a triangle "E" to 2 adjacent sides of square "sm" to make an "E-sm-E" unit (shown in green). Sew the "E-sm-E" unit to the V-shaped unit. Repeat to make 4 corner units.

6. Sew a corner unit to each corner of the center star.

7. Sew 8 triangles "E" around the block.

8. Sew a "B" triangle to each corner of the block.

Fish

1. Sew 8 diamonds "13" together to make the center star.

2. Sew a triangle "sm" to either side of a house piece "O." Repeat to make 8 units "sm-O-sm" (shown in blue).

3. Sew a "sm-O-sm" unit between diamonds "13" all around the center star.

4. Sew a diamond "5" between the "sm-O-sm" units all around the block.

5. Sew a triangle "B" to each corner of the block.

Rolling

1. Sew 8 diamonds "11" together to make the center star.

2. Sew a triangle "lg" to the top, bottom, and sides of the center star.

3. Sew a square "lg" to the corners of the center star.

4. Sew a diamond "11" to each side of a triangle "lg." Repeat to make 4 units "11-lg-11" (shown in blue).

5. Sew an "11-lg-11" unit to the top, bottom, and sides of the center star.

6. Sew a triangle "B" to each corner of the block.

SHAPES USED	BLOCK INSTRUCTIONS	ASSEMBLY DIAGRAM

Corner Half

1. Sew 8 diamonds "11" together to make the center star.

2. Sew a rectangle "D" to a triangle "lg." Repeat to make 4 units "D-lg" (shown in blue).

3. Sew a "D-lg" unit to the top, bottom, and sides of the center star.

4. Sew 4 diamonds "8" together to make a 4-diamond unit (shown in red). Add a square "C," 2 triangles "E," and a triangle "lg" to the unit. Repeat to make 4 corner star units.

5. Sew a corner star unit to each corner of the center star.

Ring-a-Round

1. Sew 4 diamonds "3" together to make a diamond unit (shown in blue). Repeat to make 16 diamond units.

2. Sew 8 of the diamond units together to make the center star.

3. Sew a square "lg" between the diamond units all around the center star.

4. Sew a remaining diamond unit between the squares "lg" all around the center star.

5. Sew a triangle "B" to each corner of the block.

Feathers

1. Sew 4 diamonds "6" together to make a 4-diamond strip (shown in blue). Repeat to make another strip with the points of the diamonds facing the opposite direction (shown in red). Sew the 2 strips together to make a feather unit. Repeat to make 4 feather units.

2. Sew the feather units together to make the center star.

3. Sew 4 triangles "xlg" together to make a large triangle-shaped unit (shown in green). Repeat to make 4 triangle units.

4. Sew a triangle unit between the feather units around the block.

5. Sew a square "39" to each corner of the block.

SHAPES USED	BLOCK INSTRUCTIONS	ASSEMBLY DIAGRAM

Basic One-Point Stand

1. Sew 8 diamonds "14" together to make the center star.

2. Sew a piece "G" to a piece "GR" as shown. Repeat to make 4 corner units.

3. Sew a corner unit to each corner of the center star.

Double Star

1. Sew 4 kites "32" together to make the center star.

2. Sew a piece "G" to a piece "GR" to make a "G-GR" unit. Sew a kite "26" to the "G-GR" unit to make a corner unit. Repeat to make 4 corner units.

3. Sew a corner unit to each corner of the center star.

Moth

1. Sew a piece "36" to a piece "Y." Add a piece "35" to make a "36-Y-35" unit (shown in blue).

2. Sew a piece "36R" to a piece "YR." Add a piece "35R" to make a "36R-YR-35R" unit (shown in red).

3. Sew unit "36-Y-35" to unit "36R-YR-35R."

4. Repeat Steps 1–3 to make 4 corner units.

5. Sew the 4 corner units together to make the block.

Enigma

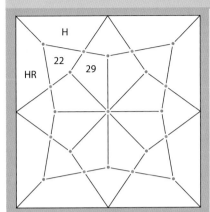

1. Sew 8 kites "29" together to make the center star.

2. Sew a kite "22" to the top, bottom, and sides of the center star.

3. Sew a piece "H" to a piece "HR" to make an "H-HR" unit. Sew a kite "22" to the "H-HR" unit. Repeat to make 4 corner units.

4. Sew a corner unit to each corner of the center star.

Whirl

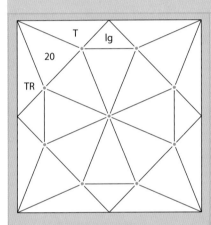

1. Sew 8 half-diamonds "20" together to make the center unit.

2. Sew a triangle "lg" to the top, bottom, and sides of the center unit.

3. Sew a piece "T" to a side of a half-diamond "20" and a piece "TR" to the other side. Repeat to make 4 corner units.

4. Sew a corner unit to each corner of the center unit.

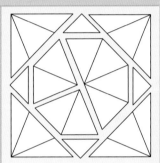

Blades

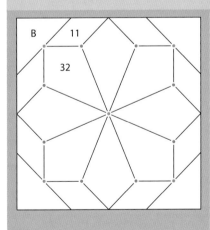

1. Sew 8 kites "32" together to make the center star.

2. Sew a diamond "11" in between each pair of kites "32" around the center star.

3. Sew a triangle "B" to each corner of the block.

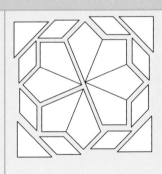

Spy

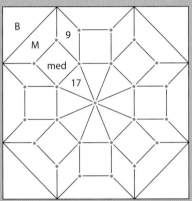

1. *Sew 8 diamonds "12" together to make the center star.*

2. *Sew a square "xlg" between each pair of diamonds "22" around the center star.*

3. *Sew a piece "U" between each pair of squares "xlg" around the block.*

4. *Sew a triangle "B" to each corner of the block.*

Castle Wall

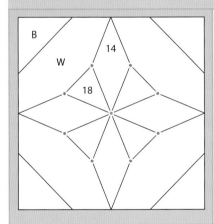

1. *Sew 8 half-diamonds "17" together to make the center unit.*

2. *Sew a square "med" to the top, bottom, and sides of the center unit.*

3. *Sew a diamond "9" to each side of a square "med" (shown in blue). Add a piece "M." Repeat to make 4 corner units (shown in red).*

4. *Sew a corner unit to each corner of the center unit.*

5. *Sew an "M" to the top, bottom, and sides of the block.*

6. *Sew a triangle "B" to each corner of the block.*

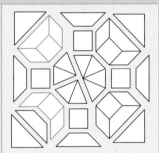

Butte

1. *Sew a half-diamond "18" to a diamond "14." Repeat to make 4 units "18-14."*

2. *Sew the 4 units "18-14" together to make the center star.*

3. *Sew a triangle "B" to a piece "W." Repeat to make 4 corner units.*

4. *Sew a corner unit to each corner of the center star.*

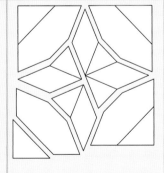

Even

1. Sew 4 half-diamonds "18" together to make a large half-diamond unit (shown in blue). Repeat to make 8 half-diamond units.

2. Sew the 8 large half-diamond units together to make the center star.

3. Sew a triangle "B" to each corner of the block.

Forbidden Fruit

1. Arrange and sew 6 diamonds "7" and 4 half-diamonds "16" into 4 strips as follows (shown in blue):

- Strip 1: 3 diamonds and 1 half-diamond
- Strip 2: 2 diamonds and 1 half-diamond
- Strip 3: 1 diamond and 1 half-diamond
- Strip 4: 1 half-diamond

2. Sew the 4 strips from Step 1 together to form a blade (shown in red). Make 5 blades and set aside.

3. To make the trunk, sew 4 diamonds "7" together to make a large diamond. Add pieces "38" and "38R" and then "37" and "37R."

4. Sew a piece "P" to a triangle "Q" and a piece "PR" to a triangle "Q" to make 2 background units.

5. Sew a background unit to each side of the trunk to make the trunk-background unit, as shown (left).

6. Sew a blade to a side of the trunk-background unit.

7. Sew the remaining 4 blades together to make the 4-blade unit.

8. Sew the 4-blade unit to the trunk-background unit.

9. Sew a triangle "B" to each corner of the tree.

BLOCK CUTTING CHART

Use the following chart to plan your cutting. First use the block piecing chart (pages 75–86) to find the shapes you'll need for your chosen blocks. Then refer to this chart to see how many of each piece to cut for your block, and to see what other blocks use the same shapes.

SHAPE	BLOCK AND # OF FABRIC PIECES
Diamond piece number: *Cut diamonds as for center star unless otherwise noted.*	
1	Two-Point-One: Cut and make 1. To make, subdivide Square E and construct center block, following instructions for Basic Two-Point Stand Star (page 9).
2	Bat: Cut 40. Peony: Cut 54.
3 *Note that you can piece 4 diamonds "3" together to make a diamond "11."*	Ring-a-Round: Cut 64.
4	Starlight: Cut 8.
5	Swallows: Subdivide Square C and cut 24 diamonds. Facets: Subdivide Square C and cut 12 diamonds. Fish: Subdivide Square C and cut 8 diamonds.
6	Feathers: Cut 32.
7	Forbidden Fruit: Cut 34.
8 *Note that you can piece 4 diamonds "8" together to make a diamond "15."*	Onstar: Cut 32. Snow Crystals: Cut 32. Carp: Cut 32. Kite Tails: Cut 8. Three Rings: Cut 16. Magical: Cut 16. Dutch Rose: Cut 16. Corner Half: Cut 16.
9	Castle Wall: Cut 8.
10	Bat: Cut 8.
11	Star Shower: Cut 8. Three Rings: Cut 8 for outside edge. Rolling: Cut 8 for center star and 8 for outside edge. Corner Half: Cut 8. Blades: Cut 8 for outside edge.
12	Ball: Cut 4. Spy: Cut 8.
13	Fish: Cut 8.
14	Basic One-Point Stand: Cut 8. Butte: Cut 4.
15	Basic Two-Point Stand: Cut 8. Facets: Cut 4.
Half-diamond piece number:	
16	Forbidden Fruit: Cut 20.
17	Castle Wall: Cut 8.
18	Butte: Cut 4. Even: Cut 32.
19	Ball: Cut 8.
20	Two-Point-One: Cut 4. Whirl: Cut 12.
Kite piece number: *Cut on lengthwise grain unless otherwise noted.*	
21	Starbrite: Cut 8. Kite Tails: Cut 4.
22	Enigma: Cut 8.
23	Starbrite: Cut 8.
24	Starlight: Cut 8.
25, 25R	Two-Point One: Cut 4 of each.
26	Double Star: Cut 4.
27	Ball: Cut 4.
28	Two-Point-One: Cut 4.
29	Enigma: Cut 8.
30	Kite Tails: Cut 8.
31	1922: Cut 4.
32	Star Shower: Cut 4. Double Star: Cut 4. Blades: Cut 8.
Irregular piece number:	
33, 33R	Fan: Cut 8 of each.
34, 34R	Fan: Cut 8 of each.
35, 35R	Moth: Cut 4 of each.
36, 36R	Moth: Cut 4 of each.
37, 37R	Forbidden Fruit: Cut 1 of each.
38, 38R	Forbidden Fruit: Cut 1 of each.
40	1922: Cut 4.
G, GR	Basic One-Point Stand: Cut 4 of each. Double Star: Cut 4 of each.

Irregular piece number:

H, HR	Enigma: Cut 4 of each.
J, JR	1922: Cut 4 of each.
K, KR	Starlight: Cut 4 of each. Starbrite: Cut 4 of each.
L, LR	Star Shower: Cut 4 of each.
M	Castle Wall: Cut 8.
N, NR	Kite Tails: Cut 4 of each.
O	Fish: Cut 8.
P, PR	Forbidden Fruit: Cut 1 of each.
Q	Forbidden Fruit: Cut 2.
R	Peony: Cut 1.
S, SR	Peony: Cut 1 of each.
T, TR	Whirl: Cut 4 of each.
U	Spy: Cut 8.
V, VR	Dutch Rose: Cut 4 of each.
W	Butte: Cut 4.
X	Magical: Cut 8.
Y, YR	Moth: Cut 4 of each.
Z	1922: Cut 4.

Square piece number:

A	Basic Two-Point Stand: Cut 4. Onstar: Cut 4. Swallows: Cut 4. Facets: Cut 4. Ball: Cut 4. Fan: Cut 4. Bat: Cut 4. Peony: Cut 4.
C	Starlight: Cut 4. Starbrite: Cut 4. Snow Crystals: Cut 4. Carp: Cut 12. Corner Half: Cut 4.
D (rectangle)	Snow Crystals: Cut 4. Corner Half: Cut 4.
39	Feathers: Cut 4.
sm	Snow Crystals: Cut 8. Carp: Cut 8. Three Rings: Cut 8. Dutch Rose: Cut 8.
med	1922: Cut 1. Castle Wall: Cut 8.
lg	Starlight: Cut 8. Starbrite: Cut 8. Star Shower: Cut 4. Rolling: Cut 4. Ring-a-Round: Cut 8.
xlg	Spy: Cut 8.

Half-square triangle piece number:

B	Two-Point-One: Cut 4. 1922: Cut 4. Three Rings: Cut 4. Magical: Cut 4. Dutch Rose: Cut 4. Fish: Cut 4. Rolling: Cut 4. Ring-a-Round: Cut 4. Blades: Cut 4. Spy: Cut 4. Castle Wall: Cut 4. Butte: Cut 4. Even: Cut 4. Forbidden Fruit: Cut 2.

Quarter-square triangle piece number:

E	Snow Crystals: Cut 8. Carp: Cut 8. Magical: Cut 16. Dutch Rose: Cut 16. Corner Half: Cut 8.
F	Basic Two-Point Stand: Cut 4. Onstar: Cut 4. Swallows: Cut 4. Facets: Cut 4. Ball: Cut 4. Fan: Cut 4. Bat: Cut 4. Peony: Cut 3.
sm	Swallows: Subdivide Square C and cut 32 triangles. Facets: Subdivide Square C and cut 16 triangles. Fish: Subdivide Square C and cut 16 triangles.
med	Magical: Cut 8.
lg	Three Rings: Cut 8. Rolling: Cut 8. Corner Half: Cut 8. Whirl: Cut 4.
xlg	Feathers: Cut 16.

HARVEST TREES

Harvest Trees, 89½″ × 104″, 2011

FINISHED BLOCK SIZE AS PICTURED: 18″ × 18″

The Forbidden Fruit block (page 61) used in this quilt is based on a Basic One-Point Stand block configuration (page 49). It has five blades, each containing six diamond patches and four half-diamond patches. The remaining (lower) part of the block is composed of a pieced trunk and the background. The Peony block (page 25) is based on a Basic Two-Point Stand block configuration (page 17). It has six blades, each containing nine diamond patches. The remaining (lower) part of the block is composed of the trunk and background.

This is a scrappy quilt—many fabrics are used in the diamond leaves, and several cream fabrics are used for the background. Dig into your stash and use up your scraps.

BLOCKS USED:

■ *Forbidden Fruit (page 61)*

■ *Peony (page 25)*

Materials

- Diamonds for leaves: A variety of fabric scraps to total 4½ yards. Scraps must measure at least 2½" × 6" for the Forbidden Fruit diamonds and 2" × 4½" for the Peony diamonds.

- Background for blocks: A variety of cream fabrics to total 3¼ yards

- Tree trunks: 1⅛ yard or a variety of brown fabrics to total 1½ yards

- Sashing and border 1: 2⅝ yards

- Border 2: 3⅛ yards

- Backing: 8⅓ yards

- Batting: 97" × 112"

- Binding: ¾ yard

Cutting

Sashing and border 1

- Cut 5 strips 4" × 54½" along the lengthwise grain for the horizontal sashing and for the border 1 top and bottom.

- Cut 2 strips 8½" × 90" along the lengthwise grain for the border 1 sides.

Border 2

- Cut 2 strips 7½" × 70½" along the lengthwise grain for the top and bottom.

- Cut 2 strips 10" × 104" along the lengthwise grain for the sides.

Binding

Cut 2"-wide strips along the bias. Join to form a continuous strip about 400" long. Fold in half, wrong sides together and press along the length of the strip.

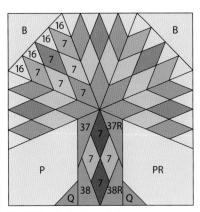

Forbidden Fruit (page 86)

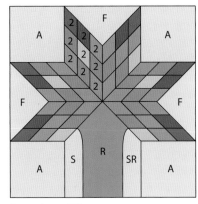

Peony (page 77)

Putting It All Together

All seam allowances are ¼". Use the template patterns provided (pullout page P1). Refer to Cutting and Piecing Tips and Techniques (pages 64–71), the block piecing chart (pages 77 and 86), and the block cutting chart (pages 87 and 88) as needed.

MAKE THE PIECED BLOCKS

Forbidden Fruit

Make freezer-paper templates for pieces "7," "16," "37," "37R," "38," "38R," "41," "B," "P," "PR," and "Q." (Either use templates 41 and Q for the trunks or piece the trunks using templates 37, 37R, 38, 38R, 7 and Q.) If you prefer, triangles "B" and "Q" may be cut directly from fabric using template measurements.

CUTTING THE PIECES FOR 6 BLOCKS

Leaf fabric

Cut 180 diamonds for the leaves using Template 7 (diamond "7").

Background fabric

- Cut 120 triangles using Template 16 (triangle "16").

- Cut 12 triangles using Template B (triangle "B").

- Cut 6 background pieces using Template P, and 6 using Template PR (pieces "P" and "PR").

Trunk fabric

- Cut 6 trunk pieces using template 41.

- Cut 12 tree foot pieces using Template Q (triangle "Q").

or

- Cut 6 upper trunk pieces using Template 37, and 6 using Template 37R (pieces "37" and "37R").

- Cut 6 lower trunk pieces using Template 38, and 6 using Template 38R (pieces "38" and "38R").

- Cut 24 trunk pieces from various trunk fabrics using Template 7 (diamond "7").

PIECING

Refer to the Block Piecing Chart (page 86) to piece 6 Forbidden Fruit blocks.

Peony

Make freezer-paper templates for pieces "2," "A," "F," "R," "S," and "SR." If you prefer, square "A" and triangle "F" may be cut directly from fabric using template measurements.

CUTTING THE PIECES FOR 6 BLOCKS

Leaf Fabric

Cut 324 diamonds from fabric scraps using Template 2 for the leaves (diamond "2").

Trunk fabric

Cut 6 trunks using Template R (trunk "R").

Background fabric

- Cut 24 corner squares using Template A (square "A").

- Cut 18 setting triangles using Template F (triangle "F").

- Cut 6 side trunks using Template S, and 6 using Template SR (pieces "S" and "SR").

PIECING

Refer to the Block Piecing Chart (page 77) to piece 6 Peony blocks.

MAKE THE QUILT TOP

1. Referring to the quilt assembly diagram, sew the blocks into 4 rows of 3 blocks, alternating the Forbidden Fruit and Peony blocks. Press.

2. Sew the rows of blocks together with the horizontal sashing. Sew the border 1 top and bottom strips to the quilt top. Press.

3. Sew the border 1 sides to the quilt top. Press.

4. Sew the border 2 top and bottom strips to the quilt top. Press.

5. Sew the border 2 sides to either side of the quilt top. Press.

FINISHING

1. Layer the quilt top, batting, and backing. Baste.

2. Quilt as desired.

3. Bind.

Quilt assembly diagram

THREE-RING MAGIC

Three-Ring Magic, 55½" × 55½", 2011

FINISHED BLOCK SIZE AS PICTURED: 12˝ × 12˝

It is important to note that the blocks used in this quilt have been modified to omit their corner B triangles; they have been replaced with center join blocks and setting triangles. The effect is to suggest the overall look of a garden maze. For added interest, the center diamond motif of some of the blocks has been fussy cut. The quilt is machine-pieced and quilted.

BLOCKS USED

Three Rings (page 35)

Magical (page 36)

Materials

■ Fabric 1 (brown batik): A variety of fabrics to total 1⅜ yards for diamonds and triangles in the blocks and for small setting triangles. Quilt pictured uses approximately ½ yard each of 3 fabrics of similar colors but different patterns.

■ Fabric 2 (pale blue print): ¾ yard for diamonds and triangles in the blocks

■ Fabric 3 (pale green print): ⅔ yard, or 1 yard of large motif to fussy cut, for diamonds in the blocks

■ Fabric 4 (dark blue print): 1¼ yards for house shapes and triangles in the blocks and for setting triangles

■ Fabric 5 (pale yellow print): 1¼ yards for small squares and border 2

■ Fabric 6 (medium blue print): 1¾ yards for triangles, center join squares, and border 1

■ Backing: 3¾ yards

■ Batting: 63″ × 63″

■ Binding: ½ yard

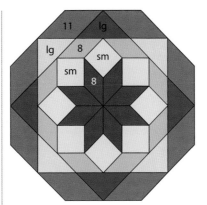

Three Rings (page 80)

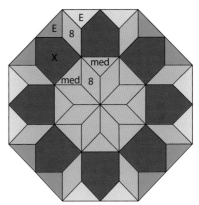

Magical (page 80)

Cutting the Center Join Squares, Setting Triangles, Borders and Binding

WOF=width of fabric

Small setting triangles fabric 1
Cut 1 strip 4⅜″ × WOF. Cut into 6 squares 4⅜″ × 4⅜″. Divide into 12 half-square triangles (triangle "a"). *

Setting triangles fabric 4
■ Cut 1 strip 13⅜″ × WOF. Cut into 2 squares 13⅜″ × 13⅜″. Divide into 8 quarter-square triangles (triangle "b").*

■ Cut 1 strip 9½″ × WOF. Cut into 2 squares 9½″ × 9½″. Divide into 4 half-square triangles (triangle "c"). *

Refer to quilt assembly diagram (page 95) for placement of setting triangles a, b and c. Triangles "b" and "c" are cut slightly oversized to allow for cutting and sewing variations.

Border 1 fabric 6
Cut 4 strips 5½″ x 56¼″ along the lengthwise grain for the top, bottom, and side borders.

Border 2 fabric 5
Cut 8 strips 2½″ × 28⅜″ along the lengthwise grain. Piece together to make 4 strips 2½″ × 56¼″ for the top, bottom, and sides.

Center join squares fabric 6
Cut 1 strip 5½″ × 22″. Divide into 4 squares 5½″ × 5½″.

Binding
Cut 2″-wide strips along the bias. Join to form a continuous strip about 232″ long. Fold in half, wrong sides together and press along the length of the strip.

Putting It All Together

All seam allowances are 1/4". Use the template patterns provided (pullout pages P1). Refer to Cutting and Piecing Tips and Techniques (pages 64–71), the Block Piecing Chart (page 80), and the Block Cutting Chart (pages 87 and 88) as needed.

MAKE THE PIECED BLOCKS

Three Rings

Make freezer-paper templates for diamonds "8" and "11." For this project, square "sm" and triangle "lg" will be cut directly from fabric, without templates.

CUTTING THE PIECES FOR 5 BLOCKS
Fabric 1

- Cut strips 1¾" wide at a 22½° angle (page 67). Cut 32 diamonds using Template 8 for the center diamonds on 4 of the blocks (diamond "8").

- Cut 4 strips 2¼" × WOF. Cut 40 diamonds using Template 11 for the third ring (diamond "11"). Note that these diamonds fit around the outer edge of the ring and so the grainline on the template indicates to cut them on a straight grain edge (Grainline Placement, page 66).

- Cut 1 strip 3⅜" × WOF. Cut into 10 squares 3⅜" × 3⅜". Divide into 20 half-square triangles for the third ring (triangle "lg").

Fabric 2

Cut strips 1¾" wide on a 22½° angle. Cut into 40 diamonds using Template 8 for the second ring (diamond "8").

Fabric 4

Cut 1 strip 3⅜" × WOF. Cut into 10 squares 3⅜" × 3⅜". Divide into 20 half-square triangles for the third ring (triangle "lg").

Fabric 5

Cut 3 strips 2¼" × WOF. Cut into 40 squares 2¼" × 2¼" for the first ring (square "sm").

Fabric 6

Cut a strip 1¾" wide on a 22½° angle. Cut 8 diamonds using Template 8 for the center block center diamond (diamond "8"). Alternatively, fussy cut 8 diamonds.

PIECING

Refer to the Block Piecing Chart (page 80) to piece 5 Three Rings blocks.

Magical

Make freezer-paper templates for diamond "8" and house piece "X." For this project, triangles "med" and "E" will be cut directly from fabric, without templates.

CUTTING THE PIECES FOR 4 BLOCKS
Fabric 1

Cut 1 strip 3¾" × WOF. Cut into 8 squares 3¾" × 3¾". Divide into 32 quarter-square triangles (triangle "E").

Fabric 2

Cut 1 strip 3¾" × WOF. Cut into 8 squares 3¾" × 3¾". Divide into 32 quarter-square triangles (triangle "med").

Fabric 3

Cut strips 1¾" wide on a 22½° angle. Cut 64 diamonds using Template 8 (diamond "8").

Fabric 4

Cut 2 strips 5¾" wide. Cut into 32 pieces using template X by inverting every alternate piece (house piece "X").

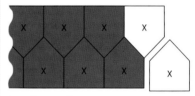

Speed cut 32 houses.

Fabric 6

Cut 1 strip 3¾" × WOF. Cut into 8 squares 3¾" × 3¾". Divide into 32 quarter-square triangles (triangle "E").

PIECING

Refer to the Block Piecing Chart (page 80) to piece 4 Magical blocks.

MAKE THE QUILT TOP

Center Three Rings Block

Sew a side of a 5½" × 5½" center join square to each corner of the center Three Rings block, starting and stopping to backstitch ¼" from the ends of the seams, as these are set-in corners.

Blocks around the Center

1. Join the 8 blocks that ring the center blocks to the remaining sides of the 5½" × 5½" squares, stopping to backstitch ¼" from the ends of the seams, as these are set-in corners.

2. Sew the remaining short horizontal and vertical areas where the sides of the blocks meet.

Extended Setting Triangles

1. Add a small half-square triangle to the outer edges of each block (triangle "a").

2. Add a quarter-square setting triangle to join the blocks (triangle "b").

3. Add half-square triangles to finish the 9-block unit (triangle "c").

Borders

1. Sew the border 1 and border 2 strips together to form a 7½"-wide border strip. Repeat to create 4 border strips.

2. Miter the corners of the strips from Step 1 at a 45° angle.

3. Sew the borders to all sides of the quilt, stopping ¼" before the ends of the seams.

4. Sew the 45° angled mitered corners together, backstitching at the beginning and end of each seam. Press.

FINISHING

1. Layer the quilt top, batting, and backing. Baste.

2. Quilt as desired.

3. Bind.

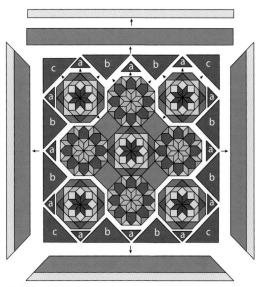

Quilt assembly diagram

Fire and Ice, 41" × 41", 2011

This quilt is made following the same blueprint as *Three-Ring Magic,* but it does not have the two outer borders. The Three Ring block is used in each corner and the center. The four remaining spaces are filled with the Magical block. The nine blocks contain either hot or cool stars. The quilt is machine-pieced and quilted.

COMMONALITIES

Commonalities, 30½" × 30½", 2011

FINISHED BLOCK SIZE AS PICTURED: 8" × 8"

I tend to get bored if all the patterns are the same and all the fabrics are the same. This piece makes use of common parts. Some of the same templates are used in all but one of the blocks. The fabrics are related but not exactly the same. One block was chosen for the grouping because it added balance to the other eight. Can you figure out which one does not share any of the templates?

BLOCKS USED

- Double Star (page 50)
- Three Rings (page 35)
- Kite Tails (page 34)
- 1922 (page 26)
- Blades (page 54)
- Butte (page 59)
- Star Shower (page 29)
- Spy (page 55)
- Ball (page 22)

Materials

- Motif centers: 9 different pieces of silk fabric, 9½" × 12" each

- Block backgrounds: 29 different pieces of tweed fabric, 12" × 15" each

- Sashing and border 1: ½ yard of silk fabric

- Border 2: ½ yard of tweed fabric

- Backing: 1⅛ yards

- Batting: 38" × 38"

- Binding: ½ yard

Cutting

Sashing and border 1

Cut 13 strips 1" × 18" wide along the lengthwise grain; piece as needed to cut the following:

- 6 strips 1" × 8½" for vertical sashing

- 2 strips 1" × 25½" for horizontal sashing

- 4 strips 1" × 31¼" for border 1

Border 2 fabric 5

Cut 8 strips 2½" × 18" along the lengthwise grain. Piece together end to end; then cut 4 strips 2½" × 31¼" for the top, bottom, and sides.

Binding

Cut 2"-wide strips along the bias. Join to form a continuous strip about 135" long. Fold in half, wrong sides together and press along the length of the strip.

Double Star (page 83)

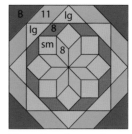
Three Rings (page 80)

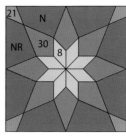
Kite Tails (page 80)

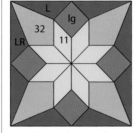
1922 (page 78)

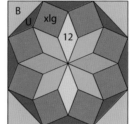
Blades (page 84)

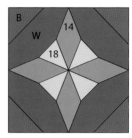
Butte (page 85)

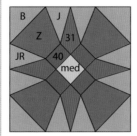
Star Shower (page 79)

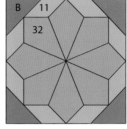
Spy (page 85)

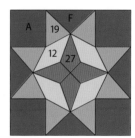
Ball (page 76)

Putting It All Together

All seam allowances are 1/4". Use the template patterns provided (pullout page P1). Refer to Cutting and Piecing Tips and Techniques (pages 64–74), the Block Piecing Chart (pages 76–85), and the Block Cutting Chart (pages 87 and 88) as needed.

MAKE THE PIECED BLOCKS

Make freezer-paper templates from the patterns provided for the following:

- Diamonds: "8," "11," "12," "14"

- Half-diamonds: "18," "19"

- Kites: "21," "26," "27," "30," "31," "32"

- Irregular shapes: "40," "U," "W," "Z," "G," "GR," "J," "JR," "L," "LR," "N," "NR"

The following pieces will be cut directly from fabric, without templates. Refer to the charts below:

- Squares: "sm," "med," "lg," "xlg," "A"

- Half-square triangles: "B," "lg"

- Quarter-square triangles: "F"

Cutting the Pieces for 9 Blocks

To take advantage of the common elements of the blocks, the cutting is by piece, not by block. Keep the cut pieces separated according to block, ready for piecing later.

DIAMONDS

Use the templates provided to cut diamonds from a short oversized strip along a 22½° edge (page 67) for the center diamonds or from a straight-grain edge (Grainline Placement, page 66) for outside edge diamonds as indicated in Chart 1 (top right).

SQUARES, HALF-SQUARE TRIANGLES, AND QUARTER-SQUARE TRIANGLES

Cut squares to exact size along the straight grain of fabric (page 68). Then divide them into half-square triangles and quarter-square triangles (pages 68 and 69) as indicated. For multiple squares and triangles, cut a longer strip and divide it into the given sizes. For measurements listed in sixteenths of an inch, estimate the center between the nearest ⅛" lines.

> **✳ tip**
>
> For cutting small increments such as ¹⁄₁₆″ divisions, I often line up with the ⅛″ markings evenly aligned across the space and make the cut.

CHART 1

Block	Use template	Cut oversized strips	Cut from template
Center diamonds to be cut from a short strip along a 22½° edge (see page 67):			
Kite Tails	8	1⅝" wide	8 diamonds
Three Rings	8	1⅝" wide	16 diamonds
Star Shower	11	2" wide	8 diamonds
Ball	12	2" wide	4 diamonds
Spy	12	2" wide	8 diamonds
Butte	14	2¼" wide	4 diamonds

Outside edge diamonds to be cut from a strip along the straight grain:

For the Three Rings and Blades blocks, do not cut Template 11 diamonds on the lengthwise grain as marked on the template. These diamonds fall along the outer edges of these blocks, so they should be cut with the straight grain running along the edge of the patches.

Block	Use template	Cut oversized strips	Cut from template
Three Rings	11	1¾" wide	8 diamonds
Blades	11	1¾" wide	8 diamonds

CHART 2

Block	Shape name on block	Cut squares		Divide into triangles	
		Exact size cut	Cut	Number of triangles per square:	Total number of triangles to cut
Squares:					
Three Rings	sm	1¹¹⁄₁₆" × 1¹¹⁄₁₆"	8 squares		
1922	med	1⅞" × 1⅞"	1 square		
Star Shower	lg	2³⁄₁₆" × 2³⁄₁₆"	4 squares		
Spy	xlg	2⁵⁄₁₆" × 2⁵⁄₁₆"	8 squares		
Ball	A	2¹³⁄₁₆" × 2¹³⁄₁₆"	4 squares		
Half-square triangles and quarter-square triangles:					
Spy	B	3³⁄₁₆" × 3³⁄₁₆"	2 squares	2 half-square	4 half-square
1922	B	3³⁄₁₆" × 3³⁄₁₆"	2 squares	2 half-square	4 half-square
Blades	B	3³⁄₁₆" × 3³⁄₁₆"	2 squares	2 half-square	4 half-square
Butte	B	3³⁄₁₆" × 3³⁄₁₆"	2 squares	2 half-square	4 half-square
Three Rings	B	3³⁄₁₆" × 3³⁄₁₆"	2 squares	2 half-square	4 half-square
Three Rings	lg	3⅝" × 3⅝"	2 squares	4 quarter-square	8 quarter-square
Ball	F	4⁹⁄₁₆" × 4⁹⁄₁₆"	1 square	4 quarter-square	4 quarter-square

HALF-DIAMONDS, KITES, AND IRREGULAR PATCHES

Use the templates provided to cut pieces from oversized strips (page 66) as specified below. For these pieces, cut the shorter measurement along the lengthwise grain.

CHART 3				
Block	Use template	Cut 2 oversized pieces		Cut from template
		Size	Number of strips	
Half-diamonds:				
Butte	18	3″ × 4″	2 strips	4 half-diamonds
Ball	19	3½″ × 7½″	2 strips	8 half-diamonds
Kites:				
1922	31	3½″ × 4½″	2 strips	4 kites
Blades	32	5½″ × 11″	2 strips	8 kites
Star Shower	32	5½″ × 5½″	2 strips	4 kites
Double Star	32	5½″ × 5½″	2 strips	4 kites
Double Star	26	3¾″ × 5″	2 strips	4 kites
Ball	27	3½″ × 4″	2 strips	4 kites
Kite Tails	30	5″ × 8″	2 strips	8 kites
Kite Tails	21	2¼″ × 4″	2 strips	4 kites
Irregular patches: See cutting from Short Strips, Step 3 (page 66)				
1922	40	3″ × 5″	2 strips	4 patches
1922	J & JR	3½″ × 8″	2 strips	4 of each (8 patches)
1922	Z	4″ × 8″	2 strips	4 patches
Double Star	G & GR	2¾″ × 10″	4 strips	4 of each (8 patches)
Butte	W	5″ × 8½″	2 strips	4 patches
Spy	U	1½″ × 9¼″	4 strips	8 patches
Star Shower	L & LR	3″ × 10½″	4 strips	4 of each (8 patches)
Kite Tails	N & NR	3″ × 7½″	4 strips	4 of each (8 patches)

Piecing

Refer to the block piecing chart (pages 75–86) to piece the 9 blocks. In keeping with the title of the quilt, the piecing order is presented by their "commonalities," not in the order that they appear in the quilt. Therefore, piece the blocks in the following order, following the piecing instructions for each block.

1922 (page 78), Double Star (page 83), Ball (page 76)

Butte (page 85), Blades (page 84), Spy (page 85)

Star Shower (page 79), Kite Tails (page 80), Three Rings (page 80)

MAKE THE QUILT TOP

Sashing

Sew the 1″ × 8½″ sashing pieces between the blocks to create 3 rows. Press.

Sew the rows together with the 1″ × 25½″ sashing strips. Press.

Borders

1. Sew the border 1 and border 2 strips together to form a 3″ × 31¼″ border strip. Repeat to make 4 border strips.

2. Miter the corners at a 45° angle.

3. Sew the borders to all sides of the quilt, starting and stopping ¼″ before the ends of the seams.

4. Sew the 45°-angled mitered corners together, backstitching at the beginning and end of each seam. Press.

FINISHING

1. Layer the quilt top, batting, and backing. Baste.

2. Quilt as desired.

3. Bind.

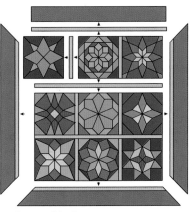

Quilt assembly diagram

EIGHT EIGHTS

Eight Eights, 61¾" × 78", 2010

FINISHED BLOCK SIZE AS PICTURED: 8" × 8"

All of the blocks were made using paper-guided piecing (pages 72–74), which allows you to piece the blocks in units and reuse the freezer-paper templates. Many blocks can be modified to suit this technique by adding seams to eliminate set-in seams and changing the order of assembly.

BLOCKS USED

- *Moth (page 51)*
- *Two-Point-One (page 21)*
- *Snow Crystals (page 30)*
- *Carp (page 32)*
- *Basic Two-Point Stand (page 17)*
- *Whirl (page 53)*
- *Even (page 60)*
- *Basic One-Point Stand (page 49)*

Materials

- Pieced blocks: A variety of fabrics to total 2 yards

- Fabric 1: 2 yards for large print blocks, pieced setting triangles, and border 2

- Fabric 2: 1⅝ yards for pieced block frames, cornerstones for sashing, and pieced setting triangles

- Fabric 3: ⅝ yard for large print block frames and cornerstones for sashing

- Fabric 4: 1 yard for sashing

- Border 1: ¾ yard

- Border 3: ¾ yard

- Backing: 5 yards

- Batting: 69″ × 85″

- Binding: ¾ yard

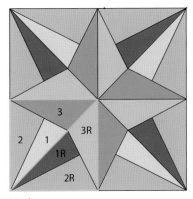

Moth

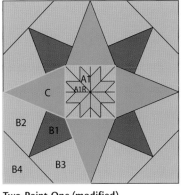

Two-Point-One (modified)

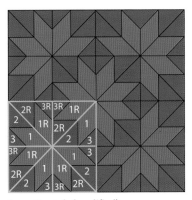

Snow Crystals (modified)

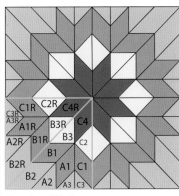

Carp (modified)

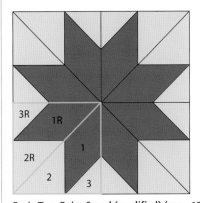

Basic Two-Point Stand (modified) (page 104)

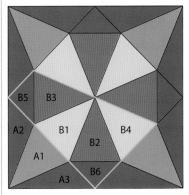

Whirl

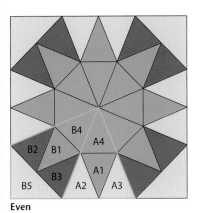

Even

Basic One-Point Stand (modified)

Cutting

Large print blocks

Cut 3 strips 8½" × width of fabric from fabric 1; cut into 10 squares, 8½" × 8½".

Block frames for pieced blocks

Cut 32 strips 1½" × 11¼" from fabric 2 along the lengthwise grain.

Block frames for large print blocks

Cut 40 strips 1½" × 11¼" from fabric 3 along the lengthwise grain.

Sashing

Cut 48 strips 2" × 10½" from fabric 4 along the lengthwise grain.

Sashing cornerstone quarter-square triangles

■ Cut 4 squares 3⅜" × 3⅜" from fabric 2; cut each diagonally twice to make 4 quarter-square triangles. You will use 14 triangles.

Sashing cornerstones

■ Cut 1 strip 2" × width of fabric from fabric 2; cut into 7 squares 2" × 2".

■ Cut 1 strip 2" × width of fabric from fabric 3; cut into 10 squares 2" × 2".

Pieced setting triangles

■ Cut 3 strips 5½" × width of fabric from fabric 1.

■ Cut 6 strips 3½" × width of fabric from fabric 2.

■ Sew the fabric 2 strips to either side of the fabric 1 strips to make 2 strips 11½" wide. Draw 2 freezer-paper templates 10⅞" × 10⅞". Cut each diagonally to make 4 half-square triangle templates. Line up the long edges of the templates along the outside edges

Quilt assembly diagram

of a pieced strip as shown. Press to hold in place and cut out. Reuse the templates to make a total of 10 pieced setting triangles from the strips.

■ Also cut 2 squares 7¹⁵⁄₁₆" × 7¹⁵⁄₁₆" from fabric 2; cut each diagonally to make 4 corner triangles.

Border 1

Cut 13 strips 2¼" × length of fabric (approximately 27"); piece as needed to cut the following:

2 strips 2¼" × 62¾" for top and bottom

2 strips 2¼" × 78¾" for sides

Border 2

Cut 11 strips 3½" × length of fabric from remaining fabric 1 (approximately ¾ yard); piece as needed to cut the following:

2 strips 3½" × 62¾" for top and bottom

2 strips 3½" × 78¾" for sides

Border 3

Cut 13 strips 2" × length of fabric 3 (approximately 27"); piece as needed to cut the following:

2 strips 2" × 62¾" for top and bottom

2 strips 2" × 78¾" for sides

Binding

Cut 2"-wide strips along the bias. Join to form a continuous strip about 288" long. Fold in half, wrong sides together and press along the length of the strip.

Putting It All Together

All seam allowances are ¼". Refer to Cutting and Piecing Tips and Techniques (pages 64–71) and Paper-Guided Piecing (pages 72–74) as needed.

MAKE THE 8 PAPER-PIECED BLOCKS

Refer to Paper-Guided Piecing to make the paper-pieced blocks. Use the template patterns provided (pullout page P2). Some blocks have been modified to suit the paper-guided piecing technique.

Moth

Use the Moth block paper-piecing template patterns to make 4 and 4 reversed freezer-paper templates.

1. Paper piece 4 units and 4 reversed units.

2. Sew each unit to a reversed unit to make 4 corners.

3. Sew 2 corners together to make a side. Make 2 sides.

4. Sew 2 sides together. Press.

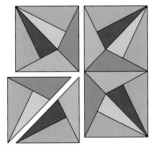

Moth block assembly

Two-Point-One

(Modified for paper piecing)

Use the Two-Point-One block paper-piecing template patterns to make 4 unit A, 4 unit A reversed, 4 unit B, and 4 unit C freezer-paper templates.

1. Use units A and A reversed, to paper piece the center block "1." Paper piece 4 units B. Cut 4 of piece "C."

2. Sew a piece "C" to each side of the center block.

3. Sew units B to corners. Press.

Two-Point-One block assembly

Snow Crystals

(Modified for paper piecing)

Use the Snow Crystals block paper-piecing template patterns to make 16 and 16 reversed freezer-paper templates.

1. Paper piece 16 units and 16 reversed units.

2. Sew each unit to a reversed unit to make 16 squares.

3. Sew 4 squares together to make a corner, referring to block assembly diagram (below). Make 4 corners.

4. Sew 2 corners together to make a side. Make 2 sides.

5. Sew 2 sides together. Press.

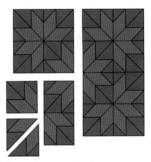

Snow Crystals block assembly

Carp

(Modified for paper piecing)

Use the Carp block paper-piecing template patterns to make 4 unit A, 4 unit A reversed, 4 unit B, 4 unit B reversed, 4 unit C, and 4 unit C reversed freezer-paper templates.

1. Paper piece 4 of each unit A, B, and C. Paper piece 4 of each A, B, and C reversed units.

2. Sew units A, B, and C together to make 4 triangle-shaped and 4 reversed triangle-shaped units.

3. Sew each triangle-shaped unit to a reversed unit to make 4 corners.

4. Sew 2 corners together to make a side. Make 2 sides.

5. Sew 2 sides together. Press.

Carp block assembly

Basic Two-Point Stand

(Modified for paper piecing)

Use the Basic Two-Point Stand block paper-piecing template patterns to make 4 and 4 reversed freezer-paper templates.

1. Paper piece 4 units and 4 reversed units.

2. Sew each unit to a reversed unit to make 4 corners.

3. Sew 2 corners together to make a side. Make 2 sides.

4. Sew 2 sides together. Press.

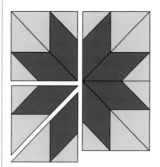

Basic Two-Point Stand block assembly

Whirl

Use the Whirl block paper-piecing template patterns to make 4 unit A and 2 unit B freezer-paper templates.

1. Paper piece 4 units A and 2 units B.

2. Sew units B together to make the center.

3. Sew units A to corners. Press.

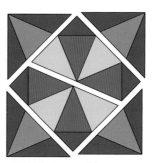

Whirl block assembly

Even

Use the Even block paper-piecing template patterns to make 4 unit A and 4 unit B freezer-paper templates.

1. Paper piece 4 units A and 4 units B.

2. Sew units A to units B to make 4 corners.

3. Sew 2 corners together to make a side. Make 2 sides.

4. Sew 2 sides together. Press.

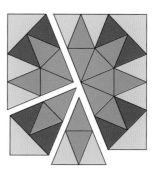

Even block assembly

Basic One-Point Stand

(Modified for paper piecing)

Use the Basic One-Point Stand block paper-piecing template patterns to make 4 unit A and 4 unit B freezer-paper templates.

1. Paper piece 4 units A and 4 units B.

2. Sew units A to units B to make 4 corners.

3. Sew 2 corners together to make a side. Make 2 sides.

4. Sew 2 sides together. Press.

Basic One-Point Stand block assembly

Make the Quilt Top

Framing

1. Miter the corners of the 1½″ × 11¼″ block frame strips at a 45° angle. Do this step with 32 fabric 2 strips and 40 fabric 3 strips.

2. Sew the fabric 2 strips to all sides of the pieced blocks and the fabric 3 strips to all sides of the large-print blocks, starting and stopping ¼″ before the ends of the seams.

3. Sew the 45°-angled mitered corners together, backstitching at the beginning and end of each seam. Press. The blocks will now measure 10½″ × 10½″.

Sashing

1. Arrange the blocks and pieced setting triangles into diagonal rows as shown in the quilt assembly diagram (page 102).

2. Sew the 2″ × 10½″ sashing pieces between the blocks and pieced setting triangles to create 6 diagonal rows. Press.

3. Arrange the 2″ × 2″ cornerstones and sashing quarter-square triangles in rows as shown in the quilt assembly diagram.

4. Sew the remaining 2″ × 10½″ sashing pieces between the cornerstones and quarter-square triangles to create 7 strips. Press.

5. Sew together the rows with the sashing strips. Press.

Borders

1. Sew the border 1, border 2 (middle), and border 3 strips together to form 2 side border strips 6¾″ × 62¾″ and 2 top and bottom borders 6¾″ × 78¾″.

2. Miter the corners of the border strips at a 45° angle.

3. Sew the borders to all sides of the quilt, starting and stopping ¼″ from the ends of the seams.

4. Sew the 45°-angled mitered corners together, backstitching at the beginning and end of each seam. Press.

Finishing

1. Layer the quilt top, batting, and backing. Baste.

2. Quilt as desired.

3. Bind.

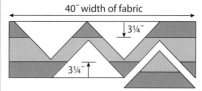

40″ width of fabric

3¼″

3¼″

Quilt assembly diagram

RUNNERS

Materials

Block motifs: A variety of fabrics to total approximately ⅝ yard, depending on chosen blocks and piecing technique

Block backgrounds: A variety of fabrics to total approximately ⅝ yard, depending on chosen blocks and piecing technique

■ Sashing: 1 fat quarter or scraps to total 18″ × 20″

■ Border: 1 fat quarter or scraps to total 18″ × 20″

■ Backing: ⅝ yard

■ Batting: 20″ × 40″

■ Binding: ⅓ yard

Cutting

Sashing
Cut 4 strips 2½″ × 8½″ along the lengthwise grain.

Border
Cut strips 2½″ × length of fabric; piece as needed to cut 2 strips 2½″ × 32½″.

Binding
Cut 2″-wide strips along the bias. Join to form a continuous strip about 100″ long. Fold in half, wrong sides together and press along the length of the strip.

✳ tip

If you choose to use silk from actual ties, it needs a little prep work first. You need to open all the seams in the tie, remove any interfacing, gently soak the tie fabric in mild soapy water, rinse, and let it dry. One tie prepared in this way will yield enough fabric to cut a variety of patches.

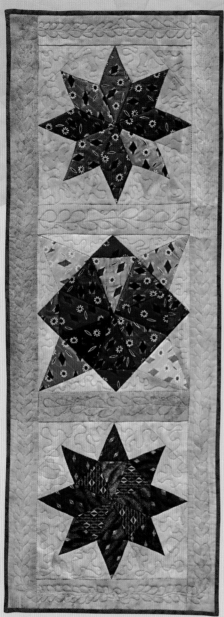

Silk Ties Runner, 12½″ × 32½″, 2011

FINISHED BLOCK SIZE AS PICTURED: 8″ × 8″

The paper-guided piecing technique was used to create the blocks of this three-block runner made from beautiful silk ties in a mixture of many different fabrics, with the emphasis on light, dark, and bright contrast.

BLOCKS USED

■ *Basic One-Point Stand (page 49)**
■ *Whirl (page 53)*
■ *Even (page 60)*

**Basic One-Point Stand is modified for paper-guided piecing (page 72). Or use your choice of any three blocks and piecing techniques.*

Putting It All Together

All seam allowances are ¼". Refer to Cutting and Piecing Tips and Techniques (pages 64–74), the Block Piecing Chart (pages 75–86), the Block Cutting Chart (pages 87 and 88), and Paper-Guided Piecing (pages 72–74) as needed.

MAKE THE PIECED BLOCKS

Decide which blocks you'd like to use for your runner. If you would like to use paper-guided piecing, check for blocks that can be made using the technique. The paper-piecing templates for the Whirl, Even, and Basic One-Point Stand blocks are provided as part of the Eight Eights project (pattern pullout page P2). Block assembly instructions for these blocks and five others can be found on pages 103-105.

For cutting, it may help to know what templates or shapes the blocks have in common, such as background patches, diamonds, kites, triangles, and so on. This information is available on the Block Cutting Chart (pages 87 and 88). Also be sure to note how many of each piece you will need and if any are reverse pieces. For example, in the block 1922, piece "J" is not symmetrical and needs a reverse piece, "JR."

> ✳ **NOTE**
>
> Any of the blocks in this book can be used in the Runners project. Just select 3 blocks in a 8" finished size. Use the Commonalities templates (pullout P1) or draft your own 8" blocks.

MAKE THE RUNNER

1. Arrange the 3 pieced blocks vertically or horizontally.

2. Sew the blocks together with the sashing strips. Sew a sashing strip to the top and bottom as well. Press.

3. Sew the border strips to the sides. Press.

FINISHING

1. Layer the quilt top, batting, and backing. Baste.

2. Quilt as desired.

3. Bind.

These four runners make a lively, scrappy grouping that was specifically created for an entryway. The wall space on either side of the door differed in both height and width, so I created a configuration of four runners that would vary in length. These are also great as table toppers or table runners.

I used silks and batiks: The centers are made from silk, and two different cream batiks frame the lively silk stars. For Basic One-Point Stand, Basic Two-Point Stand, and Whirl, I used paper-guided piecing (pages 72–74 and 103–105). For the other blocks, I backed the silk with lightweight fusible interfacing (page 65) before cutting and piecing.

Runner 1,
11¾" × 34½",
Blocks:
1922,
Kite Tails,
Blades

Runner 2,
11¾" × 23",
Blocks:
Even,
Double Star

Runner 3,
11¾" × 34½",
Blocks:
Basic One-Point Stand,
Basic Two-Point Stand,
Moth

Runner 4,
11" × 44",
Blocks: Spy,
Ball, Whirl,
Star Shower

CREATE YOUR OWN GRID

The grid I originally drew for the blocks in my first quilt using this method, *Silk Wood Blocks* (page 63), was 8" × 8", but I had to redo it in a 7¾" × 7¾" size for that specific quilt. Why such an unusual size? Because I had a piece of fabric I wanted to use, and I needed that size block or I wouldn't have enough fabric. This is one of the best things about my method—it is very adaptable, and you can make star blocks any size you want.

The lightly drawn lines shown in the illustrations below are guide lines that you will erase later. Use a light touch to make erasing the lines easier. These instructions are for the square version of the master grid, but they can be adapted to make a reference point version (page 11).

1. Create **Square A**.

  a. Draw a square the size of the finished desired block and call it **Square A** (shown in blue).

  b. Lightly draw long diagonals from corner to corner.

  c. Mark the center of the square (where the long diagonals cross).

  d. Measure and mark the center points of the square sides **A**.

2. Placing a compass point on a corner, compass measure from the corner of the square to the center of the square. Swing an arc with this measurement from each corner across each side of the square, putting tick marks where the arc crosses the side lines. Make 2 tick marks per swing. Swing an arc from each of the 4 corners, making a total of 8 tick marks. Starting at the top left of the square, number these tick marks **1** through **8**.

3. Create **Square B**.

  a. Draw short diagonal lines across the corners from **1** to **8**, **2** to **3**, **4** to **5**, and **6** to **7**. Mark dots where these lines intersect the long diagonal lines, and call the dots **B**.

  b. Connect the dots to make a square, and call it **Square B** (shown in tan).

  c. Lay a straight edge along each side of **Square B**, extending to the outer edge of **Square A**. Make tick marks where these lines intersect **Square A**, and call these marks **B**.

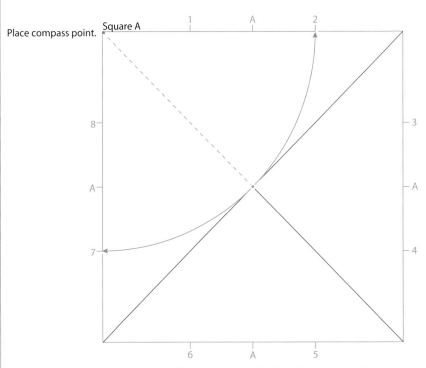

Draw Square A. Mark centers A and side points 1 through 8.

4. Create and subdivide **Square C**.

   a. Draw lines to connect points **1** to **6**, **2** to **5**, **3** to **8**, and **4** to **7**. Mark dots where the lines intersect.

   b. Connect the dots to make a square, and call it **Square C** (shown in green).

   c. Repeat Step 2 on **Square C**, but call the tick marks h rather than numbering them **1** through **8**. Call the outside corners **g** and the centers **a**. Lay a straight edge vertically and then horizontally to connect the **h** dots on **Square C**, extending to the outer edge of **Square A**. Make tick marks where these lines intersect **Square A** and call these marks **h**.

   d. Lightly draw a partial Basic Two-Point Stand star inside of **Square C**. Refer to Subdividing Square C (page 15) to learn how to use this shape.

5. Create **Square D**.

   a. Draw diagonal lines across **Square A** connecting centers A. Mark dots where they intersect the long diagonal lines.

   b. Connect the dots to make a square, and call it **Square D** (shown in orange). **Square D** is ½ the size of **Square A**.

   c. Lay a straightedge along each side of **Square D**, extending to the outer edge of **Square A**. Make tick marks where these lines intersect **Square A**, and call these marks **D**.

6. Create **Square E**.

   a. Erase all the pencil guide lines. Draw new lines connecting the **A**'s to the opposite **B** corners all around. Mark dots where they intersect each other, within **Square C**.

   b. Connect the dots to make a square and call it **Square E** (shown in purple).

   c. Lay a straightedge along each side of **Square E**, extending to the outer edge of **Square A**. Make tick marks where these lines intersect **Square A** and call these marks **E**.

7. Create **F** dots and outer marks..

   a. Draw 2 lines from each corner of **Square A** across to the nearest **B** markings on the corresponding sides of **Square A**. Mark dots where they intersect each other, just outside of **Square B**.

   b. Call the dots **F** (shown in turquoise), but do not connect them.

   c. Line up the **F** dots horizontally and vertically, extending to the outer edge of **Square A**. Make tick marks where these lines intersect **Square A**, and call these marks **F**.

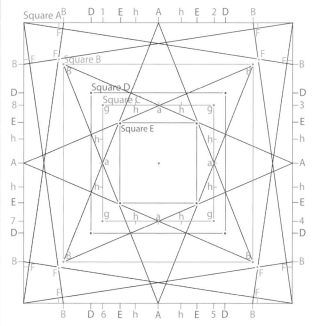

Create Square E , dots and outer marks.

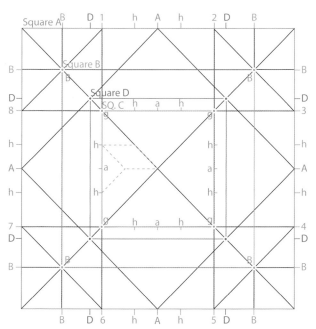

Create Square B, Square C, and Square D.
The dashed lines on this grid illustrate the useful shapes that can be drawn by Subdividing Square C (see page 15).

8. Create **Square G**.

a. Erase all the lightly-drawn guidelines. Line up a paper tape edge along one side of **Square C**, and transfer the measurement of **g** to **h** onto the tape using tick marks. Line up the paper tape along **Square A**, placing the first tick mark at the corner and the second along the **Square A** line. Make a tick mark on the **Square A** line to correspond to the second tick mark on the paper. Repeat all around **Square A** and call these tick marks **G**.

b. Line up the **G** markings horizontally and vertically, and lightly draw pencil guide lines. Place dots where these lines intersect.

c. Connect the dots to make a square, and call it **Square G** (shown in gold).

9. Create **Square H**.

a. Line up a paper tape edge along **Square C**, and transfer the measurement of **h** to **a** onto the tape using tick marks. Line up the paper tape along **Square A**, placing the first tick mark at the corner and the second along the **Square A** line. Make a tick mark on the **Square A** line to correspond to the second tick mark on the paper. Repeat all around **Square A** and call these tick marks **H**.

b. Line up the **H** markings horizontally and vertically, and lightly draw pencil guide lines. Place dots where these lines intersect.

c. Connect the dots to make a square, and call it **Square H** (shown in teal).

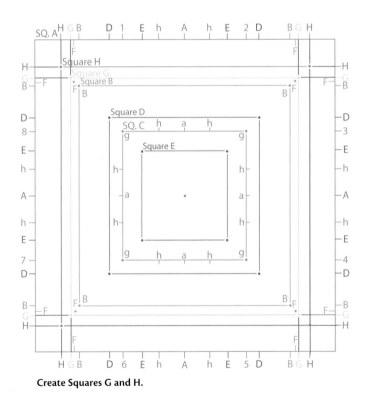

Create Squares G and H.

ABOUT THE AUTHOR

Mary Knapp is a retired biology teacher who still likes to teach, but now she teaches quilting.

The author's family consists of a supportive husband, two grown sons and their families, and a huge Newfoundland dog. All of them add to the qualities used in her quilts. The men always have an opinion and new ideas to develop. The dog forces Mary to take a break and go for a run in any weather. Many of the tips she develops are put through the troubleshooting process during those runs. These breaks also include skiing in the winter and swimming and boating in the summer in upstate New York.

Mary has taught classes and had exhibits in a variety of venues. One of her quilts was used as art for the cover of a college math textbook. She has earned numerous awards in a variety of quilt shows. Mary enjoys machine piecing because of the sharp precision it affords, but she also likes hand appliqué because of the softness. Many of her quilts that have won awards have been hand-quilted, but she also machine quilts.

Mary designed a series of quilt patterns based on lighthouses along the Great Lakes Seaway Trail, which runs along the northern border of New York State. Quilts made from these patterns are shown in the book *Shoreline Quilts* published by C&T Publishing.

RESOURCES

Sewing Machines

Bernina of America, Inc.
www.berninausa.com

Fabric

The Cotton Club
106 N. 6th, B5
Boise, ID 83702
208-345-5567
www.cottonclub.com

The Vermont Quilt Festival every June is another favorite resource. Three of my favorite vendors at the show are

Pinwheels
2006 Albany Post Road
Croton-on-Hudson, NY 10520
914-271-1045
www.pinwheels.com

Dreamcrafters Quilts
1422 State Route 37
Hogansburg, NY 13655
518-358-4285

Country Keepsakes
570-744-2246
www.countrykeepsakesonline.com

Notions

C&T Publishing

Quilter's Freezer Paper Sheets

Shape-Flex fusible interfacing

Look for these items at your local quilt or craft store, or order from www.ctpub.com.

Great Titles and Products

from C&T PUBLISHING

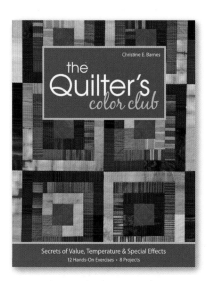

Available at your local retailer or **www.ctpub.com** *or* **800-284-1114**

For a list of other fine books from C&T Publishing, visit our website to view our catalog online.

C&T PUBLISHING, INC.

P.O. Box 1456
Lafayette, CA 94549
800-284-1114

Email: ctinfo@ctpub.com
Website: www.ctpub.com

C&T Publishing's professional photography services are now available to the public. Visit us at www.ctmediaservices.com.

Tips and Techniques *can be found at www.ctpub.com > Consumer Resources > Quiltmaking Basics: Tips & Techniques for Quiltmaking & More*

For quilting supplies:

COTTON PATCH

1025 Brown Ave.
Lafayette, CA 94549
Store: 925-284-1177
Mail order: 925-283-7883

Email: CottonPa@aol.com
Website: www.quiltusa.com

Note: Fabrics shown may not be currently available, as fabric manufacturers keep most fabrics in print for only a short time.